BEYOND BORDERS

Reflections on the Resistance & Resilience Among Immigrant Youth and Families

EDITED BY
FLAVIO BRAVO & ERIN BRIGHAM

UNIVERSITY OF SAN FRANCISCO PRESS

Published by the
UNIVERSITY OF SAN FRANCISCO PRESS
Joan and Ralph Lane Center for
Catholic Social Thought and the Ignatian Tradition

University of San Francisco
2130 Fulton Street
San Francisco, CA 94117-1080
www.usfca.edu/lane-center

Collection copyright © 2019
ISBN 978-1-949643-21-3 | paperback
ISBN 978-1-949643-22-0 | epub

Authors retain the copyright to their individual essays.

Published by the University of San Francisco Press through the Joan and Ralph Lane Center for Catholic Social Thought and the Ignatian Tradition of the University of San Francisco.

The Lane Center Series promotes the center's mission to advance the scholarship and application of the Catholic intellectual tradition in the church and society with an emphasis on social concerns. The series features essays by Lane Center scholars, guest speakers, and USF faculty. It serves as a written archive of Lane Center events and programs and allows the work of the center to reach a broader audience.

Cover: A university-bound, Latinx enjoys the Southern California sunshine during a semester abroad. Photography by Lisa Beth Anderson, a 2019 Master in Migration Studies graduate from the University of San Francisco. Lisa studies how communities tell their migration stories through photography. Her work, illustrating important journeys and poetic encounters, has appeared in textbooks, neighborhood 'zines, and the *New York Times*.

The Lane Center Series

Published by the Joan and Ralph Lane Center for Catholic Social Thought and the Ignatian Tradition at the University of San Francisco, the Lane Center Series explores intersections of faith and social justice. Featuring essays that bridge interdisciplinary research and community engagement, the series serves as a resource for social analysis, theological reflection, and education in the Jesuit tradition.

Visit the Lane Center's website to download each volume and view related resources at www.usfca.edu/lane-center

Volumes

*Catholic Identity in Context:
Vision and Formation for the Common Good*

*Today I Gave Myself Permission to Dream:
Race and Incarceration in America*

Islam at Jesuit Colleges and Universities

*Pope Francis and the Future of Catholicism in the United States:
The Challenge of Becoming a Church for the Poor*

*The Declaration on Christian Education:
Reflections by the Institute for Catholic Educational Leadership and the
Joan and Ralph Lane Center for Catholic Studies and Social Thought*

Dorothy Day: A Life and Legacy

Editor

Erin Brigham
Lane Center, University of San Francisco

Editorial Board

KIMBERLY RAE CONNOR
School of Management, University of San Francisco

THERESA LADRIGAN-WHELPLEY
Ignatian Center for Jesuit Education, Santa Clara University

CATHERINE PUNSALAN MANLIMOS
Institute for Catholic Thought and Culture, Seattle University

LISA FULLAM
Jesuit School of Theology of Santa Clara University

DONAL GODFREY, S.J.
University Ministry, University of San Francisco

MARK MILLER
Department of Theology and Religious Studies,
University of San Francisco

MARK POTTER
Newton Country Day School of the Sacred Heart, Newton MA

FRANK TURNER, S.J.
Delegate for the Jesuit Intellectual Apostolate, London

Table of Contents

Acknowledgements 7

Foreword 9
FLAVIO BRAVO

Unmasking Harmful Rhetoric and Structural
Complicity: Toward a Moral Response to Unaccompanied
Minors in the U.S. Context 13
KRISTIN E. HEYER

Schools as Sites of Refuge and Resource for
Newcomer Immigrant Youth and Families 39
MONISHA BAJAJ

Ignatian Banners of Hope and Support
for Recently Detained Immigrant Families 51
DANIELA DOMÍNGUEZ

Learning Interrupted: Deportation as an
Educational Policy Issue 71
GENEVIEVE NEGRÓN-GONZALES

The Continued Degradation of
Children's Rights in the Trump Era 85
EMILY L. ROBINSON

The Undocumented Truth: Uncovering Stories of *La Perrera*,
Trauma, Human Rights Violations, and Separation of Children
and Families Coming out of a South Texas I.C.E.
Detention Center 105
BELINDA HERNANDEZ-ARRIAGA

No Need to Fear; We're American 123
JULIO E. MORENO

Acknowledgements

We would like to thank each participant in the Lane Center's 2018 Roundtable on Immigrant Youth and Families and the following community partners who made it possible: Kino Border Initiative, Pangea Legal, Educators for Fair Consideration (now Immigrants Rising), Loyola Immigrant Justice Clinic, the Jesuit Conference of the United States and Canada, and Faith in Action (PICO). And finally, thank you to Lisa Beth Anderson who contributed her photography for the front cover.

Foreword

FLAVIO BRAVO[1]

During his historic visit to Ciudad Juárez in 2016, Pope Francis addressed the inhumane treatment of unaccompanied minors who had recently arrived at the U.S.-Mexico border. In his homily delivered to over 30,000 people, Francis reminded us that "This [humanitarian] crisis which can be measured in numbers and statistics, we want instead to measure with names, stories, families."[2] Three years later, the severity of this crisis has only heightened with the disconcerting separation of families detained at the border, while others continue to be deported from within the boundaries of the U.S. Although we are living in a time period in which more information about immigration is being shared in the daily news cycle than ever before, many of us remain confused and concerned. In the chapters that follow, professors from across the Jesuit network respond to Pope Francis's call by sharing not only the harsh realities migrants deal with, but also the resiliency of immigrant children and their families worldwide.

Given the Jesuits' long-standing commitment to upholding the inherent dignity of each human person, the *Joan and Ralph Lane*

---

1   Flavio Bravo received his MA in Migration Studies from the University of San Francisco in 2019. He previously received his BA from Loyola University Chicago in 2016.
2   Fernandez, Manny., "Pope Francis Visits U.S. – Mexico Border," *The New York* Times (February 17, 2016) available at https://www.nytimes.com/live/pope-francis-at-us-mexico-border/

Center for Catholic Social Thought and the Ignatian Tradition at the University of San Francisco holds a particularly unique responsibility as it engages in this story-telling project. Throughout the 1980's, Jesuit priests and professors at the University of Central America in San Salvador defended the rights of Central Americans displaced by El Salvador's violent civil war. Today, one would be hard-pressed to travel throughout Latin America without encountering a migrant shelter operated by the Jesuits or a sister religious community. Nonetheless, in 2008, the *Kino Border Initiative* (KBI) opened its doors in Nogales, Sonora, Mexico with a commitment to offering humanitarian aid, education, and advocacy on behalf of recently deported migrants. Each day, this Jesuit ministry serves as a witness to the widespread mistreatment and abuse of migrants at the U.S.-Mexico border.

Beyond the social ministry of KBI and the international Jesuit Refugee Service, Jesuit universities have also taken important steps toward supporting the educational pursuits and livelihoods of immigrant students and their families. In 2013, Loyola University Chicago's Stritch School of Medicine exercised an institutional act of hospitality by becoming the first medical school in the U.S. to publicly open its doors to applicants with DACA[3] status.[4] In 2014, Saint Peter's University in New Jersey announced the opening of its undocumented student resource center.[5] Loyola University Chicago undergraduate students followed suit by voting to raise their own tuition dollars in 2015 to expand financial resources for their undocumented peers who do not qualify for federal financial aid and the majority of scholarships.[6] In 2016, the *Associated Students of the*

---

3   Deferred Action for Childhood Arrivals – Executive Memo signed by President Obama in 2012
4   "Loyola University Chicago Medical School Welcomes DREAMers in Class of 2018." (Aug. 22, 2014) Available at http://jesuits.org/news-detail?tn=news-20140821092926
5   "Saint Peter's University Opens Center for Undocumented Students." (January 5, 2015) Available at http://jesuits.org/news-detail?TN=NEWS-20141219114921
6   Gonzales, Roberto G. "Lives in Limbo: Undocumented and Coming of Age in America." University of California Press, 2016, p. 234.

University of San Francisco (ASUSF) decided to allocate a portion of its annual budget each year to assist undocumented students with non-tuition dollars, most often used for the growingly expensive cost of living within the Bay Area. One year prior, in 2015, USF's School of Law launched its *Immigration and Deportation Defense Clinic* to represent unaccompanied children and migrant women with children in Northern California and the Central Valley.

Altogether, these acts of solidarity demonstrate how Jesuit institutions have strived for greater acceptance and empowerment of migrants and refugees. Contributing to this effort, the collection of essays in this book helps contextualize the intricacy and brokenness of our global migration system through a lens of history, psychology, law, education, and theology. In the first essay, Kristin Heyer from Boston College delves into Catholic migration ethics and discusses the moral and policy considerations for unaccompanied minors who seek asylum at the U.S. southern border. Then, Professor and Chair of USF's Department of International and Multicultural Education, Monisha Bajaj, reviews how schools can be sites of refuge for newly arrived immigrant and refugee youth. Writing as a clinical psychologist, Daniela Domínguez reflects on her experience accompanying 15 USF Counseling Psychology students to Puebla, Mexico and calls for greater partnership amongst national and international Jesuit institutions in order to protect the human rights of migrant children and their families.

Associate Professor of Education and Co-Chair of USF's Task Force to Support Undocumented Students, Genevieve Negrón-Gonzales, shares how deportation is an educational issue by re-telling the stories of three young people whose educational lives have been directly impacted by deportation or the threat of deportation. Emily Robinson of the Loyola Immigrant Justice Clinic at Loyola Law School, Los Angeles, offers a legal analysis of steps taken under the Trump administration to end protections for child migrants, while shifting resources so that they are treated and prosecuted as adults. Coordinator for the Master in Counseling, Marriage and Family Therapy program at USF's San José campus, Belinda Hernandez-

Arriaga draws on experiences leading a group of graduate students to McAllen, Texas and describes the harms to the mental health of immigrant children while held in detention. Finally, USF Professor of History, Julio Moreno, provides a historical breakdown of middle-class Americans and the rise of anti-immigrant groups in the U.S.

The stories, findings, and reflections on the subsequent pages should offer both valuable insight and genuine frustration. Following the three steps of the Ignatian pedagogical paradigm, which calls us to *experience, reflect,* and *act,* means that taking the time to learn about the grave injustices embedded within the fabric of the U.S. immigration system is only the first step. Most important will be the manner in which you decide to respond.

Unmasking Harmful Rhetoric and Structural Complicity: Toward a Moral Response to Unaccompanied Minors in the U.S. Context

KRISTIN E. HEYER[1]

Introduction

Significant changes for immigrant youth wrought by President Donald Trump during the first year of his presidency directly reflect his campaign rhetoric that casts immigrants and refugees as threats to the United States.[2] Trump campaigned on promises to deport

---

1 Kristin E. Heyer is Professor of Theological Ethics at Boston College. Her books include *Kinship Across Borders: A Christian Ethic of Immigration* (2012) and *Prophetic and Public: The Social Witness of U.S. Catholicism* (2006), both published with Georgetown University Press. She has also published the co-edited volumes *Public Theology and the Global Common Good: The Contribution of David Hollenbach* (Orbis Press, 2016); *Conscience and Catholicism: Rights, Responsibilities and Institutional Responses* (Orbis Press, 2015); and *Catholics and Politics: Dynamic Tensions between Faith and Power* (Georgetown University Press, 2008). She co-chairs the planning committee for Catholic Theological Ethics in the World Church.

2 I am grateful for the research assistance of Lindsay Marcellus. This essay is adapted from Kristin E. Heyer, "Toward a Moral Response to Unaccompanied Minors in the U.S. Context," in Hille Haker and Molly Greening, eds., *Unaccompanied Minor Children: Social, Legal and Ethical Perspectives* (Lexington Books, 2018); portions are adapted from Heyer, *Kinship Across Borders: A Christian Ethic of Immigration* (Washington, D.C.:

undocumented immigrants and secure the border with Mexico, a country he charged with sending its criminals, drug dealers and rapists to the United States. The administration's internal enforcement measures and accompanying rhetoric have fanned the flames of nationalism, sowed fear in immigrant communities and eroded civic life. Increased enforcement measures have contributed not only to upticks in detentions of noncriminal migrants and border deaths, but also to heightened mental health risks in immigrant communities and threats to familial well-being on both sides of the border.

As resistance to such measures has underscored, these moves threaten to harm already vulnerable asylum seekers and divide families of mixed immigration status. They also endanger the nation's deepest values and its standing in the world. In the name of safeguarding national security, further militarization of the border treats symptoms rather than causes of migration. The U.S. government already spends more on federal immigration enforcement than on all other principal federal criminal law enforcement agencies combined.[3] Moreover, since 2008, the United States has witnessed a dramatic decline in the undocumented population, and a growing percentage of border crossers have originated in the Northern Triangle countries of Central America fleeing pervasive violence and seeking not to evade arrest, but request political asylum.[4]

Since 2014, more than 200,000 unaccompanied minors have come to the U.S., the majority arriving from the Northern Triangle countries of Honduras, Guatemala and El Salvador, which remain plagued by

---

Georgetown University Press, 2012) and Heyer, "Internalized Borders: Immigration Ethics in an Age of Trump," *Theological Studies* 79.1 (March 2018) 146-164.

3 Doris Meissner, Donald Kerwin, Muzaffar Chishti, and Claire Bergeron, *Immigration Enforcement in the United States: The Rise of a Formidable Machinery* (Washington, DC: Migration Policy Institute, 2013) 9.

4 Robert Warren and Donald Kerwin, "The 2,000-mile wall in search of a purpose: since 2007 visa overstays have outnumbered undocumented border crossers by a half million," *Journal on Migration and Human Security* 5.1 (March 2017) 124-136.

organized crime and the world's highest murder rates.[5] Beyond food insecurity and family reunification, escalating violence increasingly fuels migration from these Central American communities. Migrants from El Salvador, Guatemala and Honduras cite forced gang recruitment and extortion as reasons for leaving home.[6] Given that homicides have only increased as Central American governments have implemented "iron fist" policing since 2003 (authoritarian responses to violent crime rates)—in Honduras, for example, about 70 youth have been murdered per month in recent years—many minors feel they have no other option than to flee home. Thirty percent of Central American youth are neither employed nor in school.[7]

In his 2018 State of the Union address, President Donald Trump urged Congress to close "glaring loopholes in our laws" that he charged gang members take advantage of to "enter the country as unaccompanied alien minors."[8] The administration's newly adopted measures have already attempted to alter the legal landscape for unaccompanied minors entering the U.S., however. For example, citing the threat of gangs like the one featured in his address, MS-13, President Trump has "moved to restrict special legal protections that help unaccompanied minors gain asylum, rewritten guidelines for judges in deportation proceedings involving children and opted not to renew funding for a program that had helped thousands

---

5   Office of Refugee Resettlement, "Facts and Data," (March 1, 2018) available at https://www.acf.hhs.gov/orr/about/ucs/facts-and-data.
6   Rocio Cara Labrador and Danielle Renwick, "Central America's Violent Northern Triangle," Council on Foreign Relations backgrounder (January 18, 2018) available at https://www.cfr.org/backgrounder/central-americas-violent-northern-triangle.
7   National Jesuit Conference and the Washington Office on Latin America, "Myths and Facts on the Central American Migration Surge," (June 24, 2014) available at http://www.jesuits.org/Assets/Publications/File/Myths%20and%20Facts%20on%20Central%20American%20Migration%20Surge.pdf.
8   President Donald J. Trump, "State of the Union Address," January 30, 2018, available at https://www.whitehouse.gov/briefings-statements/president-donald-j-trumps-state-union-address/.

secure legal aid."⁹ Whereas the backlog of cases in immigration court reached nearly 90,000 children in August 2017, the Department of Justice decided not to renew approximately $4.5 million in funding for Justice AmeriCorps, a program created three years ago that helped provide legal services to nearly 7,000 unaccompanied minors, citing the "loss of key leadership and inadequate performance" among the reasons for not renewing the funding.¹⁰ The administration also formally terminated the Obama-era program granting Central American minors a two-year renewable "parole" if they did not win refugee status, but had a parent already legally present in the United States.¹¹

The administration has also adjusted other internal policies to counter inherited "catch and release" practices it feared encourage unaccompanied minors to risk crossing the border, such as prosecuting sponsors (usually parents) and pursuit of "the most serious, readily provable offense" leading to federal prosecution for illegal entry rather than mere deportation. When parents are detained for federal prosecution in this way, family separation results.¹² Whereas President Trump's rhetoric suggests Central American youth migrating to the United States are chiefly male gang members, roughly one third of unaccompanied minors in 2017 were female.¹³ Sexual violence targeted

---

9   Nicole Einbinder, "How the Trump Administration is Rewriting the Rules for Unaccompanied Minors," *Frontline* (February 13, 2018) available at https://www.pbs.org/wgbh/frontline/article/how-the-trump-administration-is-rewriting-the-rules-for-unaccompanied-minors/.
10 Einbinder.
11 David Nakamura, "Trump Administration Ends Obama-era Protection Program for Central American Minors," *Washington Post* (August 16, 2017) available at https://www.washingtonpost.com/politics/trump-administration-ends-obama-era-protection-program-for-central-american-minors/2017/08/16/8101507e-82b6-11e7-ab27-1a21a8e006ab_story.html?utm_term=.c4921fd0bd63.
12 Sarah Pierce, Jessica Bolter, and Andrew Selee, *Trump's First Year on Immigration Policy: Rhetoric vs. Reality* (Washington, DC: Migration Policy Institute: 2018), 4-5.
13 Office of Refugee Resettlement, "Facts and Data," (March 1, 2018) available at https://www.acf.hhs.gov/orr/about/ucs/facts-and-data.

at Salvadoran girls, coerced relationships and gang membership has left young women with little option but to flee; moreover "only a fraction of unaccompanied minors apprehended since 2011 have confirmed gang ties."[14]

A look back at the recent peak of unaccompanied migration to the U.S. in 2014 sheds some light upon the background of the current rhetoric about security and 'illegal immigration.' This paper will attempt to scrutinize dominant narratives about unaccompanied minors' migration against a backdrop of broader diversionary rhetoric; it will help to re-contextualize their migration by noting historical and structural contexts of migration; and it will offer resources from Catholic migration ethics in terms of its attention to social sin and structural justice by way of response.

Recontextualization: The Recent History

The resonance of candidate Trump's anti-immigration rhetoric may have its roots in the recent history concerning the uptick in border-crossing of unaccompanied minors in particular. A 2014 United Nations High Commissioner for Refugees study of more than 400 unaccompanied minors found widespread experiences of violence or threats by organized-crime groups, including gangs, drug cartels, or state actors in countries of origin (48%); recruitment or exploitation by human smuggling organizations (39%); and abuse at home (22%).[15] As a result, the number of unaccompanied children crossing the U.S. border doubled annually from 2011-2014. Smuggling networks profited from these lower risk passengers who frequently turn themselves in upon crossing. After a steady decline in 2016, in

---

14 Molly O'Toole, "El Salvador's Gangs are Targeting Young Girls," *The Atlantic* (March 4, 2018) available at https://www.theatlantic.com/international/archive/2018/03/el-salvador-women-gangs-ms-13-trump-violence/554804/?platform=hootsuite.

15 United Nations High Commissioner for Refugees, "Children on the Run: Unaccompanied Children Leaving Mexico and the Need for International Protection" (Washington, DC: UNHCR, March 12, 2014).

November of 2017, the number of unaccompanied minors taken into custody rose 26 %.[16]

When an estimated 63,000 unaccompanied minors crossed into the U.S. between October 2013 and July 2014, the uptick (nearly twice the year prior) was alternately framed as a humanitarian or security crisis, adding fuel to the flame of fear-based arguments in the wider national debate about undocumented immigration. Of the group, more than 50,000 minors migrated from El Salvador, Guatemala, and Honduras. A 2013 UN Refugee Agency survey indicated that despite the threats of unscrupulous coyotes and myriad risks and costs of the journey north, the possibility that children would win asylum status via slow deportation hearings or evade authorities was preferable for many families to the threats of violence at home. Whereas some minors were placed in Health and Human Services shelters, many were put into the care of family members already living in the U.S. while they awaited their hearings; during that period, they could enroll in public schools.[17] By way of initial response, the Obama administration intensified enforcement and detention efforts and promoted public information campaigns in sending countries to discourage outflows.[18] The government opened emergency detention centers on military bases, "provided emergency legal counsel to children, accelerated the processing and deportation of migrants

---

16 Nick Miroff, "To Curb Illegal Border Crossings, Trump Administration Weighs Separating Kids from Parents," *Chicago Tribune* (December 21, 2017) available at http://www.chicagotribune.com/news/nationworld/politics/ct-trump-immigrants-parents-children-20171221-story.html.

17 Danielle Renwick, "The U.S. Child Migrant Influx," *Council on Foreign Relations* (August 28, 2014) available at https://www.cfr.org/backgrounder/us-child-migrant-influx.

18 Marc R. Rosenblum and Isabel Ball, "Trends in Unaccompanied Child and Family Migration from Central America," *Migration Policy Institute* Fact Sheet (January 2016) available at https://www.migrationpolicy.org/research/trends-unaccompanied-child-and-family-migration-central-america.

[and] provided Central American countries with $255 million for repatriation and reintegration programs."[19]

Whereas the relative dip in child and family arrivals in the fall of 2014 indicated to some that the regional migration had been resolved, more recent data indicate Northern Triangle migration pressures endure. Mexican deportations of Central Americans have markedly increased since the country implemented Programa Frontera Sur in 2014, with little deterrent effect and reports of exacerbated human rights violations of migrants in transit through Mexico to the United States. For example, criminal gangs and government officials have targeted migrants for kidnapping and extortion.[20] Critics worry the plan "outsources" the U.S. "war on migrants" and that "the model of ramping up resource extraction, militarization, and privatization threatens to worsen inequality and spur a wave of human rights violations without solving the root causes of the crisis."[21] Unless underlying conditions change, given enduring family ties across the borders, lengthy backlogs in U.S. courts and adaptive smuggling networks, Central American flows—including of unaccompanied minors—will likely persist.[22]

Given that these underlying conditions continue to endure in Northern Triangle countries from which minors flee, such as the world's highest murder rates, deaths linked to drug trafficking and organized crime, and endemic poverty, new policies and practices across the region and new considerations in the field of Christian

---

19 David M. Hernandez, "Unaccompanied Child Migrants in 'Crisis': New Surge or Case of Arrested Development?" *Harvard Journal of Hispanic Policy Policy* 27 (2014) 11.
20 Jan-Albert Hootsen, "Jesuit groups call Trump's border wall a distraction as migrants suffer," *America* (October 12, 2017) available at https://www.americamagazine.org/politics-society/2017/10/12/jesuit-groups-call-trumps-border-wall-distraction-migrants-suffer.
21 teleSUR, "Mexico Does U.S. Dirty Work Detaining Central American Children," *MintPress News* (October 25, 2016) available at http://www.mintpressnews.com/mexico-does-us-dirty-work-detaining-central-american-children/221756/.
22 Rosenblum and Ball.

ethics must address the particular needs of children on the move.[23] With the Trump administration's drastic reductions in the number of refugees the U.S. will receive and its suspension of Temporary Protected Status for several affected countries, among them El Salvador with over 260,000 beneficiaries, the U.S. risks turning its back on the vulnerable "children from neighboring countries who show up at our border with no parents and no place to turn." As Sonia Nazario worries, we may well leave those who survive the journey to make their own asylum case in court alone, i.e., without legal representation, as six in ten unaccompanied children presently do. She recounts watching "a 7-year-old stand before a judge, shaking like a leaf, because anything he said could send him hurtling back to the danger he just fled."[24] Many unaccompanied minors bear legitimate claims that could lead to legalization if they were able to navigate the nation's complex immigration and asylum laws; roughly 40% are "potentially eligible for some kind of relief from deportation."[25] Over the past five years, young defendants with legal representation "won 85% of their cases in immigration court, while those without a lawyer lost 87% of their cases."[26]

Whereas the dominant narratives either reduce the causes of the minors' entry to lax executive orders or misleading promises of

---

23 See Rodrigo Dominguez-Villegas, *Strengthening Mexico's Protection of Central American Minors in Transit*, (Washington, DC: Migration Policy Institute, 2017) available at https://www.migrationpolicy.org/news/mpi-report-amid-spike-apprehension-unaccompanied-child-migrants-mexicos-screening-housing-care and Rosenblum and Ball.
24 Sonia Nazario, "Trump's Cruel Choice: Who Gets to Stay?" *New York Times* (October 27, 2017) available at https://www.nytimes.com/2017/10/27/opinion/sunday/dreamers-children-immigration-congress.html.
25 Annie Chen and Jennifer Gill, "Unaccompanied children and the U.S. immigration system: challenges and reforms," *Journal of International Affairs* 68.2 (2015) 115+.
26 Warren Richey, "Alejandra, Age 7, is facing a judge alone. Is that due process?" *Christian Science Monitor* (November 1, 2016) available at https://m.csmonitor.com/USA/Politics/2016/1101/Alejandra-age-7-is-facing-a-judge-alone.-Is-that-due-process.

smugglers or violence and lack of economic opportunity in their countries of origin, rarely does political analysis extend to the histories of unequal relationships between sending countries and the U.S., such as its military presence in Honduras[27] and El Salvador.[28] The narratives that have framed unaccompanied minors' presence and ignored historic and structural relationships reflect the broader context of undocumented immigration in the U.S., which is also marked by diversionary myths and a focus on individual lawbreakers instead of acknowledging broader structural responsibility. Reducing immigration matters to the "illegality" of minors who cross borders alone eclipses transnational actors responsible for violent conflict, economic instability or climate change from view, much less blame. Recent administrations' enforcement strategies have focused on symptoms rather than causes of migration. The measures are framed by narratives that perpetuate myths about responsibility for irregular migration and genuine threats to national security reflective of enduring interpretive lenses.[29]

The Power of Rhetorical Framing: Narratives Old and New

Despite significantly beefed up fortification, the increase in arrivals of unaccompanied minors in 2014 rekindled fears of a "border out of control." Fewer than 48 hours after the nation collectively chanted

---

27 Joseph Nevins, "How U.S. Policy in Hondruas Set the State for Today's Mass Migration," *The Conversation* (October 31, 2016) available at https://theconversation.com/how-us-policy-in-honduras-set-the-stage-for-todays-mass-migration-65935.

28 Gene Palumbo and Azam Ahmed, "El Salvador Again Feels the Weight of Washington Shaping its Fate," *New York Times* (January 9, 2018) available at https://www.nytimes.com/2018/01/09/world/americas/el-salvador-trump.html.

29 See Heyer, "Reframing Displacement and Membership: Ethics of Migration," *Theological Studies* 73.1 (March 2012) 188-206 and "The Politics of Immigration and a Catholic Counternarrative: A Perspective from the United States," *Asian Horizons* 8.4 (December 2014) 719-737.

"USA!" for the national soccer team in the 2014 World Cup, a smaller group of Americans in Murrieta, California, coupled the same rally cry with chants of, "Return to sender," "Save our children from diseases," and "Bus illegal children to White House." The protesters employed the slogan to turn back busloads of Central American youth destined for a new detention center in their community.[30] Whether in such overtly jingoistic and racialized framing of young newcomers as particular threats, or subsequent language pitting the innocence of DACA recipients or Dreamers against the culpability of their undocumented parents, narratives shape thought and frame responses. They also help to sustain an amnesia about historic ties and to obscure social responsibilities.

The language surrounding the 2014 unaccompanied minor arrivals underscored a growing "crisis" in light of a "surge" of minors entering the country. Media images included "photos of children lying about on floors, crowded behind prison bars, or overflowing into hallways of detention facilities," further focusing attention on the dangerously porous border.[31] As David Hernandez has pointed out, such framing in terms of "crisis" and "surge" served those on either side of the immigration debate, "demonstrating an unenforced and out-of-control border for anti-immigrant forces, a cruel and rushed detention apparatus for migrant advocates, and the urgent need for comprehensive immigration reform for the Obama administration." For example, Department of Homeland Security attorneys contended that Central American refugees represented a security threat that would encourage trafficking, and that they should be treated en masse rather than as individuals. Such prosecutorial decisions led to accelerated court processes intended to deter further migrations by hastening deportations, not prioritizing just adjudication of asylum

---

30 Matt Garcia, "The Thousands of Children Fleeing Central America Have Nothing to Do with Our Ongoing Debate Over Immigration," *Zócalo* (July 10, 2014) available at http://www.zocalopublicsquare.org/2014/07/10/whats-happening-at-the-border-is-a-humanitarian-crisis-not-a-political-one/ideas/nexus/.

31 Hernandez, 11.

claims.³² Moreover, the federal government's lack of preparedness to process and provide custody arrangements for unaccompanied children as required by law magnified the sense of "crisis."

In response, two competing narratives emerged, primarily blaming "push" or "pull" factors for the crisis. Whereas a focus on "push" factors in sending countries ostensibly leads to a humanitarian frame and in many cases determining refugee categorization, the Obama administration adopted the "pull" factor narrative and consequent deterrence-based responses. Despite its expansion of border enforcement funding, information campaigns and deportation "outsourcing," such practices have not had a deterrent effect – the numbers of unaccompanied minors only temporarily dropped in 2015. If the crisis is instead "humanitarian in nature and regional in scope," the "push" narrative has explanatory value and the migrant "surge" represents, rather, a refugee flow. The "crisis" and "surge" language and adoption of the "pull" frame allowed the U.S. government and public to avoid the reality of the violence in Northern Triangle countries, its legal obligations towards refugees, and to prescind from serious consideration of its complicity in the flows or broader obligations in justice.³³

More broadly, the function of such framing rhetoric helps perpetuate dominant narratives that have long framed immigration debates in the U.S., despite rhetoric about liberty and hospitality celebrated beneath the Statue of Liberty. Policy debates have typically remained focused on social costs and security threats, in ways consonant with tropes amplified during the 2016 presidential campaign and continued following Trump's election. Its policy debates remain framed by a law-and-order lens, which casts unauthorized immigrants as willful lawbreakers, posing national security threats, including the young migrants turning themselves in

---

32 Hernandez, 11.
33 Karen Musalo and Eunice Lee, "Seeking a rational approach to a regional refugee crisis: lessons from the summer 2014 'surge' of Central American women and children at the US-Mexico border," *Journal on Migration and Human Security* 5.1 (2017) 137+.

to authorities upon arrival. Trump's internal enforcement steps follow from the politics of exclusion peddled throughout his campaign, when appeals to economic and cultural anxieties were often cloaked in nativist rhetoric. Such ongoing portrayals of undocumented immigrants and asylum seekers reflect false assumptions and facile analyses of complex challenges.

Trump billed his initial immigration order as a measure to "Make America safe again," following from the law and order mantle he adopted to distinguish his candidacy. This framework casts unauthorized immigrants as willful lawbreakers, posing national security threats. The administration's continued efforts to conflate unaccompanied minors' entrance with gang activity perpetuates this trope, yet recent studies indicate higher rates of immigration correlate with lower rates of violent and property crime.[34] The rule of law rightly occupies a privileged place in the U.S., yet a lack of accountability that marks Border Patrol procedures, and the lack of due process afforded immigrant detainees, belie this rationale.[35] The Department of Homeland Security's significant backlogs and priority "rocket" dockets in immigration courts give rise to concerns that the removal system is both inefficient and lacking in adequate safeguards. As noted, young migrants from the Northern Triangle countries flee homicide capitals where gang members murder with impunity—hence the threat driving many such migrants is precisely the breakdown of the rule of law at home.

Another script from Trump's migration platform casts newcomers as economic threats, a perception historically fueled in times

---

34　Walter Ewing, Daniel E. Martínez, and Rubén G. Rumbaut, "The Criminalization of Immigration in the United States," American Immigration Council (July 13, 2015) available at https://www.americanimmigrationcouncil.org/research/criminalization-immigration-united-states.

35　Donald Kerwin, "Rights, the Common Good and Sovereignty in the Service of the Human Person," in Kerwin and Jill Marie Gerschutz, eds., *And You Welcomed Me: Migration and Catholic Social Teaching* (Lanham, MD: Rowman & Littlefield, 2009) 93-122 at 111.

of economic downturn.[36] Beyond studies that show immigrant laborers provide a net benefit to the US economy—recent estimates indicate that DACA beneficiaries alone would contribute $460.3 billion to the U.S. gross domestic product over the next decade[37]— the detention industry profits off of irregular migrants, further confounding the "economic threat" frame. Like counterparts in Britain and Australia, the U.S. government increasingly employs multinational security companies, which have turned immigration enforcement into a growth industry. The upsurge in privatized detention has been accompanied by record profits, as well as by lawsuits based on documentation of widespread abuse and neglect. Share prices for GEO group and Corrections Corporation of America rose over 100% in the wake of the 2016 election, given the president's avowed commitment to increase incarceration of immigrants. The Administration has called for nearly doubling the number of immigrants detained to 80,000/day, and in April the White House approved plans to construct a $110 million detention center operated by GEO near Houston.[38] Detainees in GEO's Adelanto Detention Center in California staged a hunger strike and a sit-in in the summer of 2017 to protest unsanitary conditions and

---

36 Trump courted the "disaffected downwardly mobile as a key voting bloc," and some developments diminishing job security contributed to their captivity beyond this economic scapegoating. See Kenneth Himes' discussion of the plight of the "precariat" and the atomization of the work place in "The State of Our Union," *Theological Studies* 78.1 (2017) 147-170 at 148-9, 160.
37 Tom K. Wong et al, "DACA Recipients' Economic and Educational Gains Continue to Grow," Center for American Progress (August 28, 2017) available at https://www.americanprogress.org/issues/immigration/news/2017/08/28/437956/daca-recipients-economic-educational-gains-continue-grow/.
38 Michelle Sainato, "Private Prison Industry Lobbying, Profits Soar Under Trump," *The Observer* (October 27, 2017) available at http://observer.com/2017/10/geo-group-private-prison-industry-profits-soar-under-trump/.

poor medical care; three had died in the previous three months.[39] The burgeoning "immigrant industrial complex" raises questions about the significant financial stakes in the broken immigration system, diminished public oversight and accountability. Human rights groups indicate that detention has neither deterred asylum seekers nor expedited deportation and is becoming a profitable end in itself. Unaccompanied minors detained in private facilities have faced overcrowded conditions, lack of adequate medical care and food, and abuse.[40]

The Trump administration has connected economic anxieties with anxieties over cultural shifts, shaping a particular vision of "America First" that casts newcomers as threatening to a nation's identity. Tapping into the related anti-immigrant sentiment has provoked the demonization of racial, ethnic and religious minorities. Bias-related hate crimes surged following the election.[41] Where appeals to nostalgia or anxieties about rapid cultural and demographic changes may have remained more hidden or coded in the recent past, Trump's sympathy with white nationalists has brought overt racist and xenophobic fears into the open. His vulgar characterizations of migrants originating in Haiti and African nations in January 2018 further confirm this conflation. Representations of the outsider as a social menace have

---

39 Leslie Berestein Rojas, "Detainees Start Hunger Strike at Adelanto Immigrant Detention Center," *KPCC* (June 13, 2017) available at http://www.scpr.org/news/2017/06/13/72892/detainees-start-hunger-strike-at-adelanto-immigran/.

40 Anna C. Manuel and Connie de la Vega, "Detention of Unaccompanied Minors in Private Facilities," *Human Rights Advocates* report (May 2016) available at www.humanrightsadvocates.org/wp-content/uploads/2016/07/HRC-28-Children-and-Private-Detention-Centers.pdf, Melissa Del Bosque, "As Feds Lock Up More Immigrant Families, Abuse Allegations Grow," *Texas Observer* (November 4, 2014) available at http://www.texasobserver.org/growing-number-abuse-cases-immigrant-family-detention-facilities/.

41 "Post-Election Bias Incidents Up To 1,372; New Collaboration with ProPublica," *SPLC Hatewatch* (November 10, 2017) available at https://www.splcenter.org/hatewatch/2017/02/10/post-election-bias-incidents-1372-new-collaboration-propublica.

been reinvented in moments of national crisis, with the general pattern evidencing xenophobia's productive function in the national imaginary. Portrayals of immigrants as public charges or a dangerously porous border have long shaped U.S. society's collective imagination. Fear of difference—even of very young children crossing a border and offering themselves to authorities—is relatively easy to mass market, and it shapes society's imagination in powerful ways. Hence, operative lenses shaping the immigration debate can mask realities and can become surrogates for other cultural and political concerns. Christian ethics can help unmask the interests and values that drive immigration policy and its impact on unaccompanied minors in particular (when cast as a "surge" to be feared, "pulled" by misunderstandings of lax loopholes). Encounters with all migrants, including minors, signal significant dissonance between these exclusionary frameworks and the inhumane impact of recent rhetoric and measures alike. At his border mass in Ciudad Juárez on the occasion of his visit to the U.S. in 2016, Pope Francis bid listeners to measure the impact of forced migration not in numbers or statistics, but with concrete names and stories, evoking a counter-narrative to those dominating the airwaves:

> They are the brothers and sisters of those expelled by poverty and violence, by drug trafficking and criminal organizations. Being faced with so many legal vacuums, they get caught up in a web that ensnares and always destroys the poorest. Not only do they suffer poverty but they must also endure these forms of violence. Injustice is radicalized in the young; they are "cannon fodder," persecuted and threatened when they try to flee the spiral of violence and the hell of drugs, not to mention the tragic predicament of the many women whose lives have been unjustly taken.[42]

Attentiveness to such three-dimensional experiences beyond caricatures or statistics can help unmask operative narratives. Probing the complex realities behind deceptive sound bites also expands

---

42 Pope Francis, homily in Ciudad Juárez, http://en.radiovaticana.va/news/2016/02/18/pope_francis__%E2%80%98no_border_can_stop_us_from_being_one_family%E2%80%99/1209507.

consideration beyond individuals who cross borders to consider the global contexts that compel migration.

Structures of Interdependence

Restrictive measures and reductive rhetoric do not convey a sense of the complex roles historic relationships, transnational politics and economic globalization play in contemporary migration, including the patterns of unaccompanied minors on the move. Understanding immigration as "individual actions of emigrants" or asylum seekers, wherein individuals are the primary site for enforcement and responsibility, has become increasingly incompatible with transnational politics and economies.[43] Developments in social sciences and migration ethics help reorient analyses away from stopgap efforts (in the face of "surges") and toward contextual assessments of what patterns of migration reveal and demand. Understanding the geopolitical structures and systems that generate and sustain migration impact culpability and warranted responses alike.

Addressing the plight of child migrants during a U.N. Human Rights Council panel in June of 2017, Archbishop Ivan Jurkovic, Vatican observer to U.N. agencies in Geneva, not only condemned polices that criminalize and detain child migrants as "an insult to human dignity" and have "lifelong consequences on a child's development," but also detention models, themselves, as "wrongly absolv[ing] the international community from responsibilities that it regularly fails to fulfill." He called upon the international community to step up its efforts to address root causes of child migration—war, violence, corruption, poverty and environmental disasters—and to take a "farsighted approach" to integral human development for the "hundreds of millions of children who are living in appalling

---

43 Saskia Sassen, *Globalization and Its Discontents: Essays on the New Mobility of People and Money* (New York: The New Press, 1998) 6-8.

conditions."⁴⁴ This approach signals not only a "push" frame of interpretation, but it also points to the contexts in which child migration occurs, the harmful limitations of deterrent detention-only approaches, and the shared responsibility for just resolutions. These contexts are often marked by historic ties and structural interdependence.

Typically, established communities and migrants are "bound together by history, politics and economics even before the act of migration bridges the distance of geography."⁴⁵ Dynamics of employer recruitment, for example, tend to be shaped by prior bonds impacted by colonialism, military invasions, or economic ties. Saskia Sassen also highlights the increasing significance of today's "multiplying global imaginaries, which are partly a function of Western economic and media dominance and have their own way of constructing bridges."⁴⁶ In the case of the U.S., mass migration in the 1960s ensued amid its expanded economic and military activity in Asia and the Caribbean and its critical role in the development of a world economic system. Both helped create conditions that mobilized people into migrations, as well as the formation of unintended bridges to the U.S. Sassen argues these patterns indicate that measures thought to deter emigration from developing countries, such as foreign investment or the promotion of export-oriented growth, "seem to have had precisely the opposite effect, at least in the short and middle run."⁴⁷ Miguel De La Torre emphasizes the ongoing legacy of 19th and 20th-century U.S. foreign policy, expansionism and neoliberal economic strategies—

---

44 Junno Arocho Esteves, "Vatican: Failure to protect child migrants an insult to human dignity," *Catholic News Service, "Top Stories"* (June 12, 2017) available at https://cnstopstories.com/2017/06/12/vatican-failure-to-protect-child-migrants-an-insult-to-human-dignity/.

45 Silas W. Allard, "Who Am I? Who Are You? Who are We? Law, Religion, and Approaches to an Ethic of Migration," *Journal of Law and Religion* 30.2 (June 2015) 320-334 at 325.

46 Saskia Sassen, "The Making of Migrations," in Agnes Brazal and María Teresa Dávila, eds., *Living With(out) Borders: Catholic Theological Ethics on the Migrations of Peoples* (Maryknoll, NY: Orbis Press, 2016) 11-22 at 12.

47 Sassen, "The Making of Migrations," 13.

with attendant narratives—in generating migration flows from Latin America.⁴⁸

Sassen's latest research links deeper dynamics of debt servicing, extraction and land grabs to new migratory flows.⁴⁹ She argues that given "predatory" forms of advanced capitalism, opaque transnational networks, and a global governance system geared to aiding corporations, migration is far more complex an issue than one concerning nationalism versus globalism or different political theories of migration and national sovereignty.⁵⁰ Concerned with emergent migrations, she traces how such factors have expelled communities from their habitats: in the case of Central American minors entering the U.S., she probes root causes behind proximate violence broadly construed, to rapidly escalating urban violence due to the destruction of small holder rural economies resulting from land grabs and mining. Getting to the roots of such violence—without simply blaming corrupt police and criminalized traffickers or keeping gang violence "local" without interrogating its transnational dimensions and origins—traces systemic migration flows to their sources, such as the role of land grabs and mining and transnational trade agreements. In view of President Trump's focus on the threats posed by MS-13 and other transnational gangs he believes further infiltrate the country via unaccompanied minors' migration, this context-attentive approach illuminates of MS-13's origins in Los Angeles during the 1980s by refugees from El Salvador's civil war, "fueled in part by Washington," and the role of U.S. deportations in its exportation to El Salvador.⁵¹

---

48 Miguel De La Torre, *The U.S. Immigration Crisis: Toward an Ethics of Place* (Eugene, OR: Cascade Books, 2016) 151-2.
49 Saskia Sassen, "Three Emergent Migrations: An Epochal Change," *SUR File on Migration and Human Rights* 13.23 (2016) 29-41.
50 Saskia Sassen, "A Massive Loss of Habitat: New Drivers for Migration," *Sociology of Development* 2.2 (Summer 2016) 211.
51 Molly O'Toole, "El Salvador's Gangs are Targeting Young Girls," *The Atlantic* (March 4, 2018) available at https://www.theatlantic.com/international/archive/2018/03/el-salvador-women-gangs-ms-13-trump-violence/554804/?platform=hootsuite.

If dominant narratives keep the cause of violence and subsequent migration flows "local" and de-humanize newcomers according to convenient (and increasingly abhorrent) scripts, I suggest the Christian tradition's commitments shape a different story, a (counter) narrative of our common humanity, our kinship, with implications for a just immigration ethic. This ethic does not offer a meek narrative that condones open borders or an ethic of hospitality by way of charity toward vulnerable children, but a tradition steeped in human rights, a relevant notion of structural sin, and summons to shared responsibility and social justice. Christian understandings of what it means to be human radically critique pervasive exploitation and prevailing immigration paradigms that enable exclusion and abet division.

Resources from Catholic Migration Ethics

Whereas a Catholic immigration ethic is rooted in biblical injunctions to welcome the stranger, it is also borne of the tradition's teachings on universal human rights, the understanding of the political community as oriented to serve the common good, and its global rather than nationalistic perspective.[52] Its notion of social sin significantly extends responsibility for irregular migration beyond individuals who cross borders or overstay visas alone. A consideration of the social sins at play in the dynamics of irregular migration illuminates our complex complicities in injustice and the need for robust solidarity with refugees and migrants. The Catholic social tradition is rooted in a scriptural vision of the person as inherently sacred and made for community. Its principles of economic and migration ethics protect not only civil and political rights, such as freedom of conscience, but also more robust social and economic rights and responsibilities. These establish persons' rights not to migrate, or fulfill human rights

---

52 Portions of this section are developed from my "A Catholic Ethic for Immigration: Attending to Social Sin and Solidarity," *Health Progress* 98.4 (July/August 2017) 30-34.

in their homeland, and to migrate, if they cannot support themselves or their families in their country of origin.[53] Hence, in situations where individuals face desperate poverty or pervasive gang violence, the magisterial tradition supports the right to freedom to migrate so they can live free from credible fears of violence or severe want.

Beyond its foundation in human rights, the Catholic right to migrate is also rooted in the tradition's commitment to universal destination of created goods; that is, the idea that goods of the earth are generally intended for everyone.[54] Whereas the social tradition recognizes the right of sovereign nations to control their borders, this right is understood not to be absolute; its qualification by conditions of social justice warrants protection for many who remain within U.S. borders or seek entry. In the case of blatant human rights violations, the right to state sovereignty is relativized by the tradition's primary commitment to protecting human dignity (whether in its teachings on humanitarian intervention or migration). More than a decade ago, the U.S. and Mexican bishops urged both nations to address root causes of and legal avenues for migration in their joint pastoral letter. They noted the need to develop the economies of sending nations like Mexico and reduce family visa backlogs. By contrast, border enforcement has remained the primary focus of U.S. migration politics, even as it has failed to resolve the problem of a significant undocumented presence within the U.S.

Whereas the narrative of willful lawbreakers or burdensome outsiders frames the rationale behind the responses to the recent entry of unaccompanied minors, the Catholic tradition's emphasis on serving the global common good contextualizes the individual acts of migrants or refugees and underscores social dimensions of justice, interdependence, and complicity with push and pull factors

---

53 United States Conference of Catholic Bishops and *Conferencia del Episcopado Mexicano*, "Strangers No Longer: Together on the Journey of Hope" (Washington, D.C.: USCCB, 2003).

54 Second Vatican Council, *Gaudium et spes* (1965) no. 69 available at http://www.vatican.va/archive/hist_councils/ii_vatican_council/documents/vat-ii_const_19651207_gaudium-et-spes_en.html.

alike. Transnational actors responsible for violent conflict, economic instability, or climate change are eclipsed from view, much less blame. Pope Francis has repeatedly emphasized solidarity with migrants, whether in his first visit outside Rome, as Pope, to the island of Lampedusa, or his lived example returning from Lesbos with refugee families. He has lamented a "globalization of indifference" that leads to the tragedies of migrants' manipulation and their deaths. His attention to the anesthetizing effects of such indifference illuminates the structures and attitudes that harm immigrants in terms of social sin.

Distinct elements of social sin—dehumanizing trends, unjust structures and harmful ideologies—shape complex dynamics that perpetuate inequalities and influence receptivity to outsiders. Whether in forms of cultural superiority or profiteering, social inducements to personal sin in the immigration context abound. Social sin indicates how powerful narratives casting immigrants as security threats or "takers" influence our personal roles in collective actions or inaction that impact migration (such as votes in a presidential election or Congressional failures to pass a clean DACA bill or comprehensive reform). Hence, socioeconomic and political structures that lead to minors' undocumented immigration are frequently connected to the ideological blinders that obstruct hospitality to immigrants. For example, the primacy of deterrence has institutionalized security concerns rather than concerns for human rights or family unity in U.S. immigration laws; the nation's economic interests have been institutionalized in uneven free trade agreements. When concerns about national identity are distorted by xenophobia and fear, anti-immigrant sentiment and ethnic-based hate crimes surge.

Internalized ideologies make persons susceptible to myths. When bias hides or skews values, it becomes more difficult to choose authentic values over those that prevail in society. Given such unreflective dimensions of social sin, a Catholic ethic not only calls for defending human rights and providing hospitality to strangers, but also unmasking the complex structures and ideologies that abet personal complicity, preventing justice for migrating unaccompanied minors and the members of their families who are often of mixed status. Viewing immigration through the lens of individual culpability alone obscures these multileveled, subtle dynamics at play. These entrenched, intertwined patterns of social sin require repentance from idolatries that marginalize and disempower those beyond our immediate spheres of concern and borders—including the aforementioned false narratives governing perceptions of migrant children. From repentance and conscientization, we are called to conversion toward interdependence in solidarity. These shifts can occur through personal encounters and relationships that provoke new perspectives and receptivity. At the broader systemic level, nations must understand themselves as collectively responsible for the shared challenges posed by child refugees compelled to cross borders. Given these multilayered dimensions of social sin, Christian migration ethics entails not only negotiating relative duties of reception, but also addressing more diffuse and complex structures and ideologies that abet complicity in injustice and apathy. Portraying immigration through a lens of individual culpability alone obscures these multileveled, subtle dynamics at play.[55]

Pope John Paul II forwarded solidarity as the key virtue demanded in a globalized era of de facto interdependence: the social face of Christian love. David Hollenbach has proposed institutional solidarity as a necessary means of moving patterns of global interdependence from ones marked by domination and oppression to ones marked by equality and reciprocity. Institutional solidarity demands the development of structures that offer marginalized persons—including young persons—a genuine voice in the decisions and policies that impact their lives. It demands the inclusion of comprehensive sets of stakes at the decision-making table, structures of institutional accountability and transparency, and empowered

---

55 For discussions of 20th-century Christian elaborations of collective egotism and social sin can help unmask operative disvalues that harden resistance to a Christian immigration ethic, see Kristin Heyer, "Radical Solidarity: Migration as a Challenge for Contemporary Christian Ethics," *Journal of Catholic Social Thought* 14:1 (2017) 97-104 at 90-91.

participation (subsidiarity).[56] Eliciting conversion from patterns of unjust complicity calls communities beyond intermittent outreach ministry or legislative advocacy, though both remain important. The witness of churches or other institutions that provide sanctuary to vulnerable minors on the move would be strengthened by prophetic conscientization efforts that foster repentance from complicity in patterns of social sin.

Catholic groups often root outreach to unaccompanied minors in biblical imperatives of hospitality to the stranger or human dignity claims or a liberationist option for the poor and vulnerable. For example, the United States Conference of Catholic Bishops' Department of Migration and Refugee Services is the largest refugee resettlement agency in the world, and one of two agencies authorized by the U.S. Department of State to resettle unaccompanied refugee children offering foster care, family reunification and other culturally competent services since 1980.[57] Beyond the importance of hospitality and compassion for the vulnerable, however, understandings of social sin underscore susceptibility to dominant rhetoric that conflates gang member with young refugees, or indifference to the contexts generating minors' flows. These dynamics invite a response that does not begin and end with charitable outreach and refuge—the importance of which is not to be underestimated in the face of urgent need—but that extends to the responsibility to unmask misleading narratives, resist harmful policies, and recontextualize minors' migration, each of which issues social responsibilities for receiving countries like the U.S., given complicity in generating sending conditions through foreign policy and economic practices. Understanding minors arriving as kin, rather than "schemers" or threats, demands we confront the realities of violence in Northern Triangle countries and our robust obligations

---

56 David Hollenbach, *Common Good & Christian Ethics* (New York: Cambridge University Press, 2002), 225.
57 See http://www.usccb.org/about/children-and-migration/index.cfm for an overview of services offered by the US Conference of Catholic Bishops' Migration and Refugee Services and its advocacy on unaccompanied minors' behalf.

in international justice. At the very least, it requires we receive refugees at this time of increasing need, not reduce our resettlement ceiling to its lowest cap since Congress created the Refugee Resettlement Program in 1980.[58]

In closing, the harms wreaked by dominant rhetoric framing unaccompanied minors as security threats or political pawns violate fundamental standards of justice and indicate the urgency of prophetic truth-telling.[59] An approach rooted in repentance from complicity in generating displacement can help reframe the debate about Central American minors' arrivals.[60] Christian commitments to universal human rights, unmasking social sin, and restorative justice can help focus our moral responsibilities to those fleeing violence and other insecurities embedded in relational histories of unequal interdependence. A recognition by the U.S. government of the humanitarian crisis generating most of the Northern Triangle unaccompanied minor flows, on the way to a fuller sense of restoration, would at least enable us, as a nation, to adjudicate their significant need for refugee protections and employ (or in some cases, reinstate) measures to ensure refugees are not returned to persecution in these countries.[61] Moving forward, moral and policy considerations of our responsibilities to unaccompanied minors should also combat diversionary and false rhetoric, provide counsel for minors making asylum claims, enable careful deliberation of said claims rather than fast-tracking or outsourcing enforcement,

---

58 Phillip Connor, "U.S. Resettles Fewer Refugees Even as Global Number of Displaced People Grows," Pew Research Center: Global Attitudes and Trends (October 12, 2017) available at http://www.pewglobal.org/2017/10/12/u-s-resettles-fewer-refugees-even-as-global-number-of-displaced-people-grows/.

59 For a meditation on theological vocation as truth-telling see M. Shawn Copeland, "Racism and the Vocation of the Christian Theologian," *Spiritus* 2.1 (2002) 15-29.

60 A Response to "Restorative Justice as a Prophetic Path to Peace?" Plenary Address by Stephen J. Pope, *Catholic Theological Society of America Annual Proceedings* 65 (2010) at 35-42 at 38.

61 Musalo and Lee, 137+.

and work to enact meaningful comprehensive immigration reform that does not trade family reunification for merit-based points or sacrifice safeguards for those fleeing violence. The first refugee family fleeing Herod invites Christians to a solidarity with unaccompanied minors in need that avoids the lure of exculpating rhetoric and facile solutions alike.

Schools as Sites of Refuge and Resource for Newcomer Immigrant Youth and Families[1]

MONISHA BAJAJ[2]

Standing on a busy intersection in an industrial part of town, Juan,[3] a senior in high school, discusses what it's like to work as a day laborer: how to get picked out from the crowd for jobs, how to avoid getting cheated, and how scary it is to operate heavy machinery. Juan worked as a day laborer every day for a year after coming to the United States as an unaccompanied minor from Central America fleeing violence back home in Guatemala, and decided to enroll in high school just before his 17th birthday and before he aged out of the educational

---

1   This essay draws heavily on previously published articles about this research, primarily: Bajaj et al., (2017) Socio-Politically Relevant Pedagogy for Immigrant and Refugee Youth. *Equity & Excellence in Education*, 50(3), 258-274.
2   Monisha Bajaj is Professor and Chair of International and Multicultural Education at the University of San Francisco. Dr. Bajaj is the editor and author of six books, including, most recently, Human Rights Education: Theory, Research, Praxis (University of Pennsylvania Press, 2017), as well as numerous articles. She has also developed curriculum—particularly related to peace education, human rights, anti-bullying efforts and sustainability—for non-profit organizations and inter-governmental organizations, such as UNICEF and UNESCO. In 2015, she received the Ella Baker/Septima Clark Human Rights Award (2015) from Division B of the American Educational Research Association (AERA).
3   All names have been changed to protect confidentiality.

system. He still goes to look for work at the "parada"[4] on days he isn't in school or when making the rent is tight.

Seng fled from Myanmar in 2007, narrowly escaping traffickers along a dangerous journey in which she was separated from her family for months. After working in the back of a restaurant in Malaysia as an unauthorized immigrant, Seng and her family were granted asylum in the U.S. in 2011, where she entered public schools in California, speaking no English, living in poverty, and carrying with her not only the trauma of political violence in Myanmar that forced her family to flee, but also difficult memories from the migration process. Four years later, and working almost every day after school in the back of a restaurant late into the night to help support her family, she graduated among the top of her class, securing a scholarship to attend a local four-year state college. Seng chose a major that would also allow her to work in Myanmar, given her goal to one day go back and live there.

Aasif left Afghanistan because, between the drug lords, the Taliban, and the U.S.-led drone strikes, he and his friends could not even play soccer without fear of violence and death. An 11th grader, he learned English and is on track to graduate next year. Aasif wants to go back and see his grandmother again, and he dreams of becoming the President of Afghanistan some day after he finishes college and when things "settle down back home."

These are three snapshots of the numerous stories of youth migrants to the United States. Juan, Seng, and Aasif all arrived to Northern California and found their way to Oakland International High School, a public high school for newly arrived immigrant and refugee youth. This essay will explore the realities of newcomer immigrant and refugee youth and how schools and social service providers can best serve this population, particularly amidst a precarious political climate in the U.S., and globally, that heightens the vulnerability of immigrant communities. In order to situate the realities of immigrant and refugee youth and their families, I will first provide some context of migration followed by examples of how one school has innovated

---

4   A gas station or corner where day laborers gather to be hired for work.

to address the needs of their student population drawing from data collected through a three-year qualitative case study I carried out along with graduate students from the University of San Francisco (USF) and Oakland International High School (OIHS). Each of the dimensions discussed highlights key insights and lessons for educators and social service providers working with immigrant youth and families.

Migration in Global and Local Contexts

Globally, some 245 million people have migrated from their country of birth to another propelled by an unequal global political economy, violent conflict, and/or environmental crises (U.N., 2016). Whether in Europe, the Middle East, sub-Saharan Africa or North America, societies that receive migrants and refugees grapple with discourses of "deserving-ness" to distinguish those who receive assistance, and those who do not (Holmes & Castañeda, 2016). The countries with the highest refugee and immigrant populations tend to be those closest to sites of extreme conflict and unrest; for example, during the brutal Syrian civil war that has been ongoing since 2011, more than half of the pre-war population (22 million) has been displaced with six of those eleven million fleeing to other countries.

While most of the Western media offers inordinate coverage of the "migrant crisis" in Europe or North America, the reality is that Syrian refugees by and large seek safety closest to home in places such as Turkey, which hosts over three million; Lebanon, which hosts over 2 million, comprising 30% of their population; and Jordan that hosts over one million. Approximately one million refugees from Syria have applied for asylum in all of Europe since 2011, and approximately 20,000 have been settled in the United States and 40,000 in Canada; amidst the severity of the humanitarian crisis and the need for resettlement, anti-immigrant and nativist policies have been proposed and/or implemented in many of these national contexts. The first and second 2017 travel bans introduced by U.S. President Donald

Trump—which commentators have also called "Muslim bans" based on his virulent Islamophobic statements that led up to their announcements—barred any and all migration from Syria. Such efforts, and a retreat from providing aid and resettlement to those in acute need, undermines the premise of international humanitarian law and the human rights architecture advanced after the creation of the United Nations immediately after World War II in 1945.

This chapter focuses on schools within the U.S., with insights for contexts globally. It is useful to explore the history of attitudes towards migration in this national context to understand current policies. In the U.S., narratives about desirable and undesirable immigrants have long pervaded political discourse, ranging from xenophobic and restrictive immigration policies in the 19th and 20th centuries to contemporary discussions of building border walls, increased scrutiny for foreign visitors, and the denial of entry altogether to individuals from certain Muslim-majority nations.

Newcomer Youth in California

Across the U.S., immigrants and refugees comprise an average of 13 percent of the population—27% of the California population is foreign born (U.S. Census, 2011)—with increasing numbers of recently arrived youth entering public schools as one of the few public institutions that is free, compulsory, and intended to be open to all regardless of documentation status. Because of this, schools are often the primary point of contact between immigrant families and the state, and an opportune location for information and resources to be centralized; yet, newcomer immigrant and refugee youth have some of the highest dropout rates of all students in the U.S. (up to 40%) given higher poverty levels, limited English proficiency, and other obstacles to persistence in school through high school graduation (Sugarman, 2015).

While public high schools in the U.S. are increasingly compelled to focus on the distinct needs and realities of these 'newcomer' youth, particularly in the wake of the politicization of their presence in schools and communities, few teacher education programs offer any courses or skills for working with this population. Some school districts have specific programs in mainstream public schools to serve these populations, and some have also established entire schools that focus on recently arrived youth, with additional time for English language learning, psychosocial support for students experiencing trauma through the migration and resettlement process (Birman et al., 2008), and services for families.

OIHS, which is part of a larger national network (the Internationals Network for Public Schools) that has helped establish dozens of schools nationwide specifically to serve newcomer English language learners, defines 'newcomers' as immigrant and refugee youth who have arrived to the U.S. within the previous four years. The Network partners with districts to create these non-charter, public schools, and each district has different policies around how teachers are hired and what additional supports are provided. The Network also assists its schools in identifying outside sources of funding that can off-set supplemental services that are often needed for this population of students.

The following sections of this chapter highlight three of the many innovative approaches that OIHS engages in as part of its stated role as a "full-service community school."[5] My co-researchers (Amy Argenal & Melissa Canlas) and I have termed the school's approach one of socio-politically relevant pedagogy (SPRP), building on the concepts of culturally responsive (Gay, 2000) and culturally relevant pedagogy that have been discussed in educational scholarship (Howard, 2003; Ladson-Billings, 1994, 1995). SPRP recognizes that youth—such as Juan, Seng and Aasif mentioned above—lead lives marked by transnationalism through their own experiences as

---

5   Oakland Unified School District defines Community Schools as those that "leverage community partnerships and resources so our campuses become hubs of support and opportunity for students, families and community members. By working with the community in this way, schools become better equipped to tap into the unique talents and gifts of every student, teacher, and staff member in our district, and can better break down barriers to student achievement." From https://www.ousd.org/CommunitySchools

migrants, often to more than one country before coming to the U.S., and who remain connected to two or more societies in a variety of ways. SPRP first encourages a cultivation of critical consciousness around interconnections between local and global issues, human rights, and the unequal circumstances under which migration occurs. This happens both within and outside the classroom. SPRP also includes the creation of formal and informal avenues for reciprocal learning between families/communities and schools. The recognition of the knowledge, resilience and cultural wealth of their communities (Yosso, 2005) must inform how schools operate and reflect students' realities. Third, within SPRP, attention is paid to the material conditions of students' and families' lives through the coordination of services and resources that support the learning process and exhibit care for students' whole selves and their families. Interestingly, this model aligns well with the vision of Spiritual Exercises of Ignatius for Jesuit education:

> The familiarity of the teacher with the student's actual life provides a context for building a shared and authentic relationship. According to the International Commission on the Apostolate of Jesuit Education, context includes a teacher's knowledge of 'family, peers, social situation, the educational institution itself, politics, economics, cultural climate, the ecclesial situation, media, music, and other realities.' [T]hrough experience of the real world—the world outside the classroom, where theory and praxis meet—students begin to consider how their emotional responses… affect their intellectual understanding.

With alignments to other educational philosophies, SPRP, when paired with a community school model where there is express commitment to go beyond the walls of the school to engage communities, can offer important resources to both immigrant students and their families, as the following sections will illustrate.

Engaging with Community

OIHS—a school with approximately 400 students from thirty-five different countries—has created opportunities for educators and staff to learn from students and their communities, while at the same time supporting their academic achievement, English language proficiency and progress towards graduation. As a public high school, but one connected to a national network of schools serving newcomer immigrant youth and families, the school has fundraised to have a community-school program manager who creates partnerships and opportunities for reciprocal learning and social services to be located on the school's campus. For example, once a month, a mobile food bank from the county comes to the school and offer students and their families a chance to access groceries, at no cost, to supplement health and nutrition in their homes (95% of students at the school qualify for free and reduced-price lunch, one indicator of socio-economic hardship). The school liaises with legal services providers to provide low- and no-cost legal services to students who may be unaccompanied minors, unauthorized migrants, or face other legal obstacles. The school also has a classroom designated for parents and community members to learn English, computer skills, or attend workshops on different issues or topics.

Once a year, the school hosts a "community walks professional development day" where educators and staff learn from students and their families about their backgrounds. Teachers and staff members visit students' communities, are introduced to important landmarks and cultural centers, meet with community leaders, and engage in discussion. In 2016, for example, seven simultaneous walks took place on the same day focused on diverse communities such as Yemeni, Afghan, Burmese, and Central American immigrants. Students on the unaccompanied minors walk, for example, showed a clip of "La Bestia" (the dangerous train many migrants take through Mexico on their journey north) from the movie, *Sin Nombre*, and then, shared stories about their own journeys across the border, riding the train, catching food from kind strangers alongside the railroad tracks, and watching helplessly as others fell off the train during their journey (Bajaj & Suresh, 2018). Yemeni students had participants on their walk partake in a circle about Islamophobia and its impact on their lives; after the discussion, students and families led the participants to a local mosque to attend prayer there. The community walks always include lunch at a community location or home, and end with a circle back at OIHS, during which staff members can debrief their experiences and reflect on their learnings with each other (Bajaj & Suresh, 2018). Community walks center students' lived realities and offer a holistic picture of how their academic lives fit into the larger picture of their often-precarious migration, current socio-economic realities, and the assets of their communities in supporting them as they pursue an education. OIHS' community walks offer a lesson in cultural humility (Tervalon & Murray-Garcia, 1998) and reflective practice needed by educators and social service providers when working with populations with diverse realities and histories of often-traumatic migration.

Adaptive Curricula for Complex Times

The classroom is where OIHS's primary goals of academic attainment and English language learning are centralized. As such, rather than having only one period of English language instruction per day, the school has English language goals integrated into the teaching of every subject throughout the school day. And as a school that accepts students year-round, there are often vastly different language levels and abilities within a single classroom. Classrooms have language and content area goals posted on the walls, and are comprised of tables for group work with multiple languages being utilized and translated in small groups at all times for comprehension.

There are many curricular examples of how the teachers seek to cultivate students' critical consciousness and awareness of global citizenship, and this section highlights just a couple. In the summer of 2015, two teachers of the 9th and 10th grade classes (which were grouped together heterogeneously), developed an inter-disciplinary unit across science and history related to issues of water use and scarcity. Rather than focusing solely on the state-wide issues of drought and water use in California, the teachers together decided to develop a unit that would have students research water collection, use, and management in their home countries, and develop a presentation in their home language directed at someone in their families; as the teachers instructed, "imagine you are presenting this information to your grandmother." The students brought in photos of the people their presentations were tailored to (photos of cousins, parents, and grandparents were assembled into a collage near the front corner of the classroom), developed these presentations in their native languages, and then, as a last step, translated their work into English in language groups and with the teachers' help, and delivered these presentations to the class. In their presentations, students discussed how they collected water in their home countries, analyzed inequalities in terms of access to water in rural and urban areas, and examined differences between water use in their home countries and the U.S.

OIHS has several forms of assessment beyond the required statewide exams, including comprehensive portfolio projects all seniors have to complete, and the encouragement of student work that responds to the needs of the community; for example, in November 2016, seniors developed and delivered presentations to younger students, in their native languages, about the 2016 election and implications for unauthorized migrants or students from Muslim-majority countries that were affected by the new administration's policies. This collective component of acquiring and demonstrating mastery of content knowledge infuses the ways that teachers approach curriculum and pedagogy.

Many students have transnational identities and connections that include academic and professional goals beyond just the learning of English and the passing of state-wide exams. The range of goals varied from attending community college or four-year universities, to obtaining a full-time job upon completion of high school, to continuing to support family back home, to returning home, if possible, to contribute to one's country. The school does not just focus on the English language acquisition, but creates a caring academic environment that can meet the diverse needs of the students and their communities. For example, one Guatemalan student was part of a book drive for libraries in her home country, and Seng, a Burmese young woman highlighted in the introduction to this essay, discussed choosing a major for college that would best allow her to go back and work there in the future. Such transnational identities necessitate that curricula, pedagogy, counseling and other school approaches attend to students' complex and multidirectional aspirations (Bajaj & Bartlett, 2017). Most teachers at OIHS, in general, do not force an assimilationist agenda on students in contrast to the literature that has noted that many educators and social service providers in marginalized communities often seek to "save" their students and engage deficit narratives about students' communities. A key takeaway from this approach is to support immigrant and refugee youth to meet their academic requirements and learn English, while also supporting their transnational civic engagement as members of diasporic global communities.

Focus on Well-Being

> The first time I came to school, Coach Ben asked me, "Do you want to play soccer? Here, we have practice Tuesday and Thursday." That helped me to stay in school. It was hard for me in the beginning to stay in school, but to have a person telling you that you belong in this community, that really helped." -Jose, unaccompanied minor from Central America, 12th grader at OIHS (as cited in Bajaj & Suresh, 2018)

Trauma—whether acute or ongoing—is a particularly difficult challenge that impedes students' ability to focus and engage in academic endeavors at school (Birman et al., 2008). OHIS provides various counseling services, from social service agencies to interns from graduate programs, to ensure that counselors with understandings of the students' backgrounds and languages are rotating through the school weekly to serve students. Counselors speak Spanish, Arabic and other languages in order to best understand the students they are working with. Coping with anxiety, stress, violence, or sexual assault in the past, during migration, or upon arrival to the U.S. are important components of attending to students' well-being. Often, the communities that students come from consider seeking mental health services as taboo; having such services as part of one's schoolday facilitates students receiving the assistance and care needed.

Within a student population made up entirely of newcomer students, many of whom are unaccompanied minors, refugees, asylees, and students with interrupted formal education (SIFE), integrating a trauma-informed approach at OIHS is essential to building successful relationships with students. The school's professional development is tailored to foster staff understanding of students' cultures and communities, as mentioned above, but administrators have also made a concerted effort to ground their collective work in an understanding of how trauma affects the brain and learning. Within the school, adults (such as Coach Ben mentioned above) strive to make students feel safe, welcome, and trusted in big and small ways. The Wellness Center, established in 2016, is open throughout the day for drop-in visits by students who need help with social service applications, health appointments, or who just need a snack or a socio-emotional break (Bajaj & Suresh, 2018). Trauma-informed approaches have increasingly informed education and understandings about health and well-being; in many schools, however, limited funding, space, and training impedes students accessing the services and supports they need. One take-away from this research is to ensure that past and current trauma be considered and adequate resources be provided to help youth and families heal and grow.

Concluding Thoughts

This essay reviewed three ways in which one school that serves newly arrived immigrant and refugee youth employs strategies for persistence and completion, socio-emotional supports and engaging families to be a resource for the community. Whether educators or social service providers working with immigrant and refugee communities, several lessons emerge including:

> (1) the whole context of youth's lives shapes their current experiences and attention to their material, emotional, academic, and socio-political needs can make programs more effective;
>
> (2) a sense of belonging and community in programs offers youth an important counterpoint to larger narratives that frame them as outsiders;
>
> (3) many youth continue to experience trauma or hardship in the U.S. (not just in home countries and in the migration journey) and deficit or savior narratives limit their ability to navigate such realities; and
>
> (4) relevant and engaging curricula that speak to students' lives within and outside the classroom prepare them holistically for present and future pursuits whether in the U.S. or transnationally.

Creating spaces of belonging, support, and opportunity for any group, and especially for immigrant youth and families, offers necessary refuge from both larger xenophobic discourses and violence directed at these communities. Such spaces can offer actual resources required to integrate into a new society and are necessary, especially when geopolitical unrest back home may have been caused by earlier meddling or intervention by the host country itself (e.g., El Salvador, Iraq, Yemen, etc.). Schools as sites of refuge can provide a framework in which to situate our work as scholars, practitioners, and educators committed to human rights and social justice.

Ignatian Banners of Hope and Support for Recently Detained Immigrant Families

Daniela Domínguez[1]

The solidarity which binds all men together as members of a common family makes it impossible for wealthy nations to look with indifference upon the hunger, misery and poverty of other nations whose citizens are unable to enjoy even elementary human rights. The nations of the world are becoming more and more dependent on one another and it will not be possible to preserve a lasting peace so long as glaring economic and social imbalances persist.[2]

Families from Central America's Northern Triangle— Guatemala, El Salvador, and Honduras, are sometimes forcibly displaced from their native land due to the immediate risks associated with violence,

---

1   Dr. Daniela Domínguez is a licensed psychologist, licensed clinical counselor, and author of several articles in academic and scientific journals. She has a special interest in social justice concerns, multiculturalism, and immigration issues. Dr. Domínguez provides counseling services to families impacted by President Trump's 'zero-tolerance' immigration policy, and she volunteers at a migrant respite center in McAllen, Texas where she engages in crisis intervention.

2   Vatican Archives, Mother and Teacher, *Mater et Magistra* # 157, St. John XXXIII, 1961. http://w2.vatican.va/content/john-xxiii/en/encyclicals/documents/hf_j-xxiii_enc_15051961_mater.html

forced gang-recruitment,[3] political unrest, absolute poverty, and human rights violations.[4] From the moment migrants depart from their home country to pursue international protection, economic opportunities, and "freedom" in the US, they embark on a dangerous and arduous journey with serious threats across Mexico. These threats include extortion, kidnappings, sexual assault, torture, human trafficking, robbery, injury, and homicide. In many cases, the cruel conditions that impact migrants are related to organized crime, often with the involvement of Mexican agencies and armed forces. Upon arrival to US ports of entry, migrant families, who are seeking international protection, often experience long delays in the processing of their asylum claims by Customs and Border Protection (CBP). Desperate to find immediate safety, scarred by the traumatic experiences encountered during their journey, and often unaware of the complexities of the asylum process, migrants cross the US border without authorization from the US government. Hoping to discourage all unlawful border crossing to the US, on May 7, 2018, the Trump administration adopted a "zero-tolerance" policy that prosecuted all unlawful entry, making no exceptions for asylum-seekers or migrants traveling with children. Although federal judge Dana Sabraw ordered the "zero-tolerance policy" to be discontinued on June 26, 2018, the detrimental effects of this "policy" persist today. According to recent reports from the Department of Homeland Security, the Trump administration has separated 81 children from their families since the end of the "zero-tolerance" policy.[5]

---

3   Manuel Paris et al. *Vulnerable but not broken: Psychosocial challenges and resilience pathways among unaccompanied children from Central America.* New Haven, CT: Immigration Psychology Working Group, 2018.

4   "Sharing the Journey," Kino Border Initiative, accessed on October 1, 2018. https://www.kinoborderinitiative.org/annual-report/

5   Geneva Sands, "81 Children Separated at Border Since Trump's Executive Order on Dividing Families," CNN Politics, https://www.cnn.com/2018/12/06/politics/immigrant-family-separations-children-border-undocumented/index.html

In this essay, I argue that while aggressive immigration enforcement practices have denigrated, dehumanized, and inflicted pain on migrant families for decades, President Trump's "zero-tolerance policy" has promoted exclusionist attitudes that have aggravated anti-immigrant sentiments and perpetuated the abuse of power by immigration officers against vulnerable migrant communities. I emphasize that the criminalization of families seeking international protection, as well as the forced separation of children from their parents, are inhumane, heartless, and have serious psychological consequences on migrants. I also stress that in reaction to this humanitarian crisis, Jesuit institutions and other faith-based organizations must continue to speak out, announce their support for human rights, protest the violence against migrant communities at the US/Mexico border, and firmly confront oppressive forces within US immigration detention facilities. Additionally, I present the case of our artistic team, a group of students and faculty members of a Jesuit university, who offered support to migrant families through meaningful artistic banners that communicate love, grace, compassion, generosity, and the social doctrine of the Catholic Church.

The information reviewed in this manuscript focuses primarily on the experiences of Central American migrant families, which is the largest group of migrants impacted by President Trump's "zero-tolerance policy." To offer context in terms of my positionality as an author and creator of the artistic project described in this manuscript, I begin by drawing on personal experiences to explain why immigration, art, and a commitment to Jesuit values, are central elements of my personal and professional work. I subsequently review legal, historical, and psychological information to describe and explain the unprecedented aggression that migrants experience in the Trump era. In the last portion of the manuscript, I share the ways in which our artistic team, a group of faculty members and students, demonstrated a commitment to Jesuit values by designing three artistic banners aimed to change the hearts and minds of people at two US/Mexico borders. I conclude with practical recommendations for Jesuit universities, which may be interested in expressing cross-border solidarity through art initiatives.

Personal Background; The Importance of Art

In light of family tradition, I received a hand-embroidered shawl from my grandmother before I moved to the United States. "Abuelita[6]" knit vibrant Aztec Dahlia flowers that stretched from the bottom corner of the shawl to its neck. A strong, indigenous Mexican matriarch, she invested countless hours designing a colorful and uniquely patterned garment that represented my upcoming journey to the US. She explained that during and after migration, she expected me to continue growing into a determined, humble, and hard-working woman loyal to her roots, cultural background, and faith formation. I understood the profound meaning of my grandmother's symbolic shawl and how the Dahlia flowers represented growth and hope rather than fear. Her shawl not only helped me feel her unwavering love and unyielding support, but it also made me aware of the wholesome power that art has to influence hearts and minds.

With the understanding that art has transformative power, I started creating fabric banners to protest the violation of human rights during my graduate studies in Counseling Psychology. Some of my banners sought to demonstrate resistance against the Defense of Marriage Act[7] and "Don't Ask Don't Tell;[8]" policies that impacted the psychological well-being of members of marginalized communities. Today, in my capacity as licensed psychologist and educator at a Jesuit university (i.e., the University of San Francisco), I volunteer at a migrant respite

---

6 Grandma
7 H.R. 3396--104th Congress: Defense of Marriage Act. (1996). In GovTrack.us (database of federal legislation). Accessed September 2, 2018, from http://www.govtrack.us/congress/bill.xpd?bill=h104-3396
8 United States Department of Defense, "Report of the Comprehensive Review of the Issues Associated with a repeal of "Don't ask, don't tell," (2010), https://www.loc.gov/item/2011507489/

center that is managed by Catholic Charities to offer support services (e.g., case management and crisis intervention) to migrant families recently released by Immigration Customs Enforcement (ICE) in McAllen, Texas. I have heard the testimonies of recently detained migrants and have witnessed the pain of family members who are suffering the psychological consequences of forced family separation. My work with migrant families at the migrant respite center has inspired me to continue to use art to challenge President Trump's "zero-tolerance policy" and any future legislative actions that violate the human rights of migrant children and their families.

Feeling inspired, in collaboration with a colleague and a group of students at USF, I recently implemented an artistic initiative for social change titled Ignatian Banners of Hope and Support for Recently Detained Immigrant Families. This initiative involved organized action at the local level to create a ripple effect beyond the walls of our Jesuit institution. Before I describe this art initiative in detail, it is essential that I provide an overview of the Trump administration's "zero-tolerance policy" to provide context as to why our artistic team believes that demonstrating resistance to aggressive immigration enforcement practices through art is critical.

President Trump's Zero-Tolerance Policy

The Trump administration is using aggressive immigration enforcement at the US/Mexico border to "remove as many non-citizens as quickly as possible."[9] One example of such aggressive immigration enforcement practices is President Trump's "zero-tolerance" policy. This policy prosecutes all unlawful entry to the US, making no exceptions for asylum-seekers or migrants traveling with children. From the time President Trump announced the "zero-

---

9 Jennifer Chacón, "Immigration and the Bully Pulpit." *Harvard Law Review* 130, no. 7 (2017): 243–68. Accessed October 30, 2018. https://harvardlawreview.org/2017/05/immigration-and-the-bully-pulpit/2.0-85019146878&site=eds-live&scope=site&custid=s3818721.

tolerance policy" through June 2018, the day when federal judge Dana Sabraw ordered the policy to be discontinued, Border Patrol officers referred 2,262 adults traveling with children to the Justice Department for prosecution.[10] Approximately 3,000 children under the age of 18 years old, were separated from their parents and placed in detention facilities.

The debate surrounding the "zero-tolerance policy" has created an atmosphere of hostility between supporters and critics of President Trump's recent executive orders. Supporters of the current administration's "zero-tolerance policy" argue that President Trump intends to protect and ensure the stability and security of Americans. They indicate that as the leader of a free nation, he has every right to control migration flows and US borders. They reject statements by critics that President Trump has failed to consider children's rights, human rights, and refugee law without regard to moral and humanitarian considerations. Immigrant rights activists, on the other hand, have proposed that President Trump's "zero-tolerance policy" fails to address the root causes of migration, which include past and present US policies that have contributed to the psychosocial and political upheaval taking place in one of the most violent regions in the world, the Northern Triangle.[11] They add that the "zero-tolerance policy" addresses only the "symptoms of the migration phenomenon,"[12] and that without taking action to provide migrants

---

10 Ron Nixon, "Migrant Families Who Enter at Legal Ports Are Rarely Separated, Customs Officials Say," *New York Times,* July 9, 2018, https://www.nytimes.com/2018/07/09/us/politics/customs-border-protection-family-separations.html
11 Rocio Labrador, and Danielle Renwick, "Central America's Violent Northern Triangle," last modified June 26, 2018, https://www.cfr.org/backgrounder/central-americas-violent-northern-triangle.
12 "Strangers No Longer : Together on the Journey of Hope : A Pastoral Letter Concerning Migration," Conference of Catholic Bishops, last modified January 22, 2003, http://www.usccb.org/issues-and-action/human-life-and-dignity/immigration/strangers-no-longer-together-on-the-journey-of-hope.cfm

with relief from root causes, migration to the US will persist, and ill-informed policies will continue to be created.

As a critic of President Trump's zero-tolerance policy, I propose that although non-citizens have endured the fear of detention, deportation, and family separation for decades, the messages of enforcement severity and hateful speech embraced by this administration have fueled a new climate of fear among migrant families and migrant children.[13] While the Obama administration practiced enforcement discretion by prioritizing the deportation of non-citizens who had committed a previous criminal offense rather than families and children,[14] President Trump has targeted unauthorized immigrants often without regard to their criminal background, risk profile, or family composition. During the Obama years, asylum seekers were not held in immigration detention unless they were considered to be public safety threats and risks. Instead, asylum seekers were administratively placed into removal proceedings, asked by the Department of Homeland Security to appear at their immigration hearings, and in some cases, later released into the US interior.

In the Trump era, however, all individuals who cross the border without authorization, regardless of whether they are asylum seekers or migrants with children, are apprehended between US ports of entry and are often criminally prosecuted for unlawful entry. When apprehended, migrant children are often placed in facilities that are inadequate to accommodate their basic needs (e.g., bathing, eating, and sleeping), which in turn impacts their psychological and physiological well-being as I discuss next.

---

13   Daniela Domínguez, "Counseling Psychology Students Working with Mixed- Immigration-Status Families in the Trump Era." Manuscript under review at the *International Journal for School-Based Counseling*.
14   Michael J. Sullivan and Roger Enriquez, "The Impact of Interior Immigration Enforcement on Mixed-Citizenship Families," *Boston College Journal of Law & Social Justice* 36, no. 33 (2016): 33-57, http://lawdigitalcommons.bc.edu/jlsj/vol36/iss1/3

The Impact of Aggressive Immigration Enforcement on Migrant Children

Migrant children are susceptible to psychological, physiological, and behavioral problems, resulting from traumatic experiences that may have occurred in their country of origin, during their migratory journey, while apprehended at detention facilities,[15] and in some cases, as a result of parent-child separation caused by prosecutory decisions. Children who were apprehended and taken to detention facilities may face intrusive questions, and their bodies, documents, testimonies, and stories are subject to strict examinations, which further exacerbates their stress levels. In the case of 3,000 children (under age 18) who were separated from their parents by immigration officers under the "zero-tolerance policy" and taken to facilities managed by the Department of Health and Human Services, it is likely that the toxic stress (i.e., extreme, prolonged, and repetitive stress) they experience/d may have a long-lasting impact on their health and development. In a CNN interview, Delfina Ismelda Paz Rodriguez and her daughter Ashley, two migrants from El Salvador, shared their experiences,

> The conditions … were awful. I was unwell and I couldn't sleep. I think that I had a nervous breakdown because of what I was going through. The officers yelled at us constantly and insulted us. For example, they told us that we were filthy. It was psychological torture.[16]

Health experts from the American Academy of Pediatrics, the American College of Physicians, and the American Psychiatric Association have indicated that the strong and prolonged emotional reactions in children caused by migration processes, as well as abuses and human rights violations occurring within detention facilities

---

15 Manuel Paris et al. *Vulnerable But not Broken: Psychosocial Challenges and Resilience Pathways Among Unaccompanied Children from Central America.* (New Haven: Immigration Psychology Working Group, 2018), 7-100.
16 Ray Sanchez, Sheena Jones, Dave Alsup and Keith Allen, CNN, "The Chill of Detention: Migrants Describe their Experiences in US custody, July 9, 2018, https://www.cnn.com/2018/07/07/us/separated-families-detention-conditions/index.html

(e.g., abuse of power by immigration officers against migrant families)[17] result in toxic stress, which could impact the development of children's brain architecture.[18] These experts indicate that because toxic stress affects impulse and emotional control, it is not surprising that children in detention centers display frequent crying, aggressive behavior, self-harm, changes in diet, sleep deprivation, withdrawal, sadness, guilt, anger, and hopelessness. Expert Victoria E. Kress, a professor of Counseling at Youngstown State University, explained,

> The research is clear that the longer the parents and children are separated, the more likely the child is to experience prolonged stress reactions such as anxiety and depression. Separation from parents, especially under stressful circumstances, can lead to attachment disruptions and a host of mental health problems. For children, traumatic events can lead to the development of post-traumatic stress disorder and other mental health disorders; these experiences can impact a child and haunt them throughout their lives and even lead to transgenerational trauma or trauma that is transferred from one generation of trauma survivors to future generations of children.[19]

As described in the former paragraph, even if children are ultimately reunited with their parents, the severe consequences of forced family separation remain. This statement is supported by research suggesting that these harmful consequences include feeling abandoned, isolated, fearful, traumatized, and depressed.[20] According to a recent report

---

17   National Public Radio, "What We Know: Family Separation And 'Zero Tolerance' at the Border, last modified June 19, 2018, https://www.npr.org/2018/06/19/621065383/what-we-know-family-separation-and-zero-tolerance-at-the-border

18   Lindsey Tanner, "'Toxic Stress': How Family Separation May Alter Kids' Brains," last modified June 28, 2018, https://www.nbcconnecticut.com/news/national-international/Family-Separation-Affect-Kids-Brains-486793591.html

19   Josie Rhodes Cook, "Psychologists Detail 'Irreparable Harm' Done to Separated Immigrant Kids, last modified June 19, 2018, https://www.inverse.com/article/46094-toxic-stress-child-psychology-immigrant-family-separation

20   Hector Adames, and Nayeli Chavez-Dueñas. *Cultural Foundations and Interventions in Latino/a Mental Health: History, Theory, and Within-group Differences* (New York: Routledge, 2017).

published by a number of psychologists, migrant children who are "victimized, re-victimized, unprotected, and neglected in their basic needs, and who do not receive prompt [clinical] interventions," may suffer serious psychological conditions.[21] These psychologists emphasize the importance of children receiving culturally and developmentally appropriate clinical services while they are in US immigration detention centers and immediately after their release into the interior of the US.

With the knowledge that the physiological and psychological impact migrants suffer as a result of aggressive immigration enforcement practices in the Trump era is serious and concerning, I propose that new psychosocial services, community initiatives, and training programs must be urgently designed to support migrant families and their children. In the next section, I discuss how a group of students and faculty members at the University of San Francisco (USF) demonstrated their commitment to Jesuit values by designing three artistic banners aimed to change the hearts and minds of people at two US/Mexico borders.

Our Project; Ignatian Banners of Love, Hope, & Solidarity

> In human society one man's natural right gives rise to a corresponding duty in other men; the duty, that is, of recognizing and respecting that right. Every basic human right draws its authoritative force from the natural law, which confers it and attaches to it its respective duty. Hence, to claim one's rights and ignore one's duties, or only half fulfill them, is like building a house with one hand and tearing it down with the other.[22]

---

21 "Sharing the Journey," Kino Border Initiative, accessed on October 1, 2018. https://www.kinoborderinitiative.org/annual-report/
22 John, Pope. "Pacem in Terris." *God and the Moral Order*, no. 37 (July 1963). 146–147. doi:10.1080/00396336308440402. http://w2.vatican.va/content/john-xxiii/en/encyclicals/documents/hf_j-xxiii_enc_11041963_pacem.html

A couple of days after President Trump announced the implementation of his "zero-tolerance policy," I traveled to Puebla, Mexico with 15 Counseling Psychology students and one colleague, to advance my understanding of the cultural, environmental, and economic stressors specific to Mexican families impacted by forced migration. Our team of students and faculty learned from the lived experiences of children impacted by their parents' forced migration to the US and actively listened to their stories of survival; narratives of grief, trauma, and resilience. During this trip, we also witnessed the ways in which children suffer great devastation by their separation from parents who have undertaken their migration journey.

After my return to the US from Mexico, I learned from our 15 students that their immersion experience in Puebla had opened their eyes and hearts to the trauma, violence, and abuse experienced by migrant families prior to migration, during their migration journey, and after migration. Conversely, I heard from students who were unable to travel to Puebla (i.e., Counseling Psychology students who remained in the US) that after learning through media outlets about the injustices and structural violence migrant children and their families experienced as a result of President Trump's zero-tolerance policy, they felt called to serve migrant populations. I believe that our students' "call" to serve was reflective of their commitment to USF's Jesuit mission.

In conversation with different Counseling Psychology students, I became aware of the fact that our Counseling Psychology program needed a variety of consciousness-raising and social justice activities that could offer more students the opportunity to engage with migrant communities, even if "solidarity" was provided from a distance. I asked myself, "Are there other ways in which we, faculty and students, can demonstrate our fidelity to our Ignatian values and commitment to social justice without having to physically travel to communities in need?" In other words, can accompaniment with migrant communities be offered from a distance and indirectly? I invested time reflecting on this question and subsequently designed what I believe to be a project that is a wellspring for creativity, grace, and hospitality. During the practice of this artistic initiative, students engaged with each other, with their own heart, and with migrant communities from a distance.

It is vital for me to point out that although face to face contact continues to be my preferred way of engaging with migrant communities, I also recognize that powerfully hands-on art projects, such as fabric or canvas banners, have the strength to communicate our sincere care for migrants and their families even if direct access to them is not possible.

The Creative Process

Ignatian Banners of Hope and Support for Recently Detained Immigrant Families is an artistic project that was approved by the USF School of Education and funded by the USF Jesuit Foundation. Following approval for the initiative, I distributed a flyer with a description of the event and invited students, faculty, and staff to participate. The flyer explained that a canvas banner would be created by USF students and faculty members to communicate our desire for cross-US/Mexico-border solidarity. This artistic event was offered across three USF campuses: USF San Francisco, USF Sacramento, and USF Santa Rosa.

Approximately 100 students participated in all three events. Fifteen of them were responsible for delivering the banners, in the company of one faculty member (i.e., the author), to two US/Mexico borders. By encouraging participation in various USF campuses, we created a wave of solidarity that sparked a spirit of love and communion between students, faculty members, and migrant communities.

Two Teams; The Artists and the Delivery Team

Two teams were arranged for the successful completion of our artistic initiative. The first team was in charge of painting the banners, and the second team was responsible for delivering the banners to two different borders. Both teams would partake in acts of resistance, hospitality, and solidarity; the first through indirect acts of resistance and the second through direct contact with communities in need. The first team's objective was to create colorful, bold, and handmade canvas banners with lasting images and compelling messages that would uplift people's spirits. Because the banners were meant to include simple graphics, anyone regardless of artistic talent could participate in the initiative.

While the first team consisted of students from diverse cultural backgrounds, racial identities, socioeconomic statuses, and sexual and gender identities, the second team (i.e., the delivery team) consisted of LatinX Spanish-speaking students. LatinX Spanish-speaking students were selected because their linguistic and cultural understanding and proficiency would facilitate their "encounter" with migrant families.

Banner Materials

I purchased different acrylic paint colors and a premier linen canvas roll (72" by 6 yards). From one roll, we created three banners of different sizes. Canvas was used for practical purposes; we needed an artistic display that could be foldable for easy transportation across state lines and around the border. Easily foldable material was used in case our delivery team needed to disperse quickly for safety reasons.

In addition, I purchased 100 lightweight and durable foam paint brushes (dimensions 1 x 2.1 inches) and 20 different colors of acrylic paint, including fluorescents and metallic colors. The use of different colors provided the opportunity for students to attach meaning and emotions to paint. While some students sketched out their design in pencil first, others used the foam brushes to letter directly with paint. I purchased this project's art materials at a local art store in San Francisco.

Artistic Procedure

We held three different events on three different days at three different college campuses. When the students arrived, they sat in a circle around the canvas banner. Before selecting their paint colors and foam brushes, together, we began reading the poem "borderbus" by Juan Felipe Herrera, a Chicano Poet Laureate of the United States. Selected by one of our students, this poem introduces the listener to two "hermanas" (i.e., sisters) who are in a bus, heading from their native country, Honduras, to the US border. The poem presents the struggle, pain, and tribulations encountered by the sisters during their migratory journey. Although we know "borderbus" does not fully capture the stories of all migrants, I believe it personalized the migrant experience and ignited powerful empathy in our students.

After the poem was read, my colleague and I harnessed our knowledge of counseling skills to create a safe space where students could process their emotional reactions to their "encounter" with these "hermanas." In addition, students were able to voice their opinions, ask questions about aggressive immigration enforcement practices, and inquire about their impact on migrant children and their families. Subsequently, students were asked to engage with the poem individually, examine their own position, and craft a powerful and nourishing message on the canvas banner. Because opportunities for processing, reflection, and discernment were offered, students were able to clarify their intention and vision when working on the banner.

Once the three banners were fully painted, they were strategically placed by our delivery team at two different borders. The locations in which these banners were placed were selected in consultation with staff at temporary migrant shelters (e.g., Desayunador Salesiano & Catholic Charities). In collaboration with these agencies, a strategic decision was made to place the banners on both sides of the border to symbolize cross-border solidarity. One banner was placed in the Playas of Tijuana in Mexico, and two banners were placed in the Rio Grande Valley in Texas.

I am proud to say that our three banners communicated love, grace, compassion, generosity, and the social doctrine of the Catholic Church. In the next section, I discuss the relationship between our artistic initiative and our commitment to Jesuit values throughout the completion of our project.

Our Artistic Initiative's Commitment to Jesuit Values

> As an unborn child he [Jesus] went from Nazareth to Bethlehem. As a child refugee he went to Egypt. As a preacher he travelled the roads of Galilee. His seemingly final journey was to travel up Calvary carrying the heavy wooden beam of a cross.[23]

In September 2017, Pope Francis launched the "Share the Journey" campaign in which he calls on all of us to welcome migrants arriving in unfamiliar and strange terrains, and emphasizes that hospitality is especially important considering the traumatic experiences migrants endure during their migratory trajectory. In a similar spirit, Former Jesuit Superior General Peter-Hans Kolvenback encourages Jesuit universities to commit to their neighbors and the world; he indicated, "The measure of Jesuit universities is not what our students do but whom they become and the adult Christian responsibility they will exercise in future towards their neighbor and the world."[24] I believe that our artistic initiative answers the call by Pope Francis to provide, in the spirit of peace and reconciliation, relief for migrants who are desperately seeking support, and aims to meet the expectations that former Jesuit Superior General Peter-Hans Kolvenback has for Jesuit institutions of higher learning.

---

23 "Easter 2018 message by Cardinal Luis Antonio Tagle," Caritas, accessed October 1, 2018. https://www.caritas.org/2018/03/easter-message-by-cardinal-luis-antonio-tagle/
24 "Forming Thoughtful, Committed Citizens," *Conversations on Jesuit Higher Education* 51, no. 10 (Spring, 2017), http://www.conversationsmagazine.org/web-features/2017/11/22/forming-thoughtful-committed-citizens

I also believe that our project aligns with the Jesuit Conference's commitment to cross-border solidarity and their position that Jesuit institutions must stand with migrants and oppose the structural and systemic injustices that lead to forced migration. The Jesuit Conference has indicated that to be agents of social change and "good examples," we must receive immigrants, refugees, exiles, and the persecuted from around the world to provide them with a safe haven.[25] They explain that even if social action unleashes controversy or strong reactions among supporters of the "zero tolerance policy," Jesuits must always be guided by reason and faith. They argue that if we are in fact guided by reason and faith, support to economically poor and marginalized migrants is urgently necessary. Our project— *Ignatian Banners of Hope and Support for Recently Detained Immigrant Families*— sought, through faith, reason, and creativity, to transform students into bold artists and courageous protesters that communicate love to migrant communities, even if that means unleashing strong reactions from supporters of the "zero-tolerance" policy. Our artistic initiative was designed with Jesuit values in mind, and this commitment is also demonstrated in the title of our project.

The Selected Title of Our Artistic Initiative

I titled the project *Ignatian Banners of Hope and Support for Recently Detained Immigrant Families* in honor of St. Ignatius. St. Ignatius clearly explained that "if the church is not marked by caring for the poor, the oppressed, the hungry, we are guilty of heresy."[26] Fr. Aloyious Mowe, the International Director of Advocacy and Communications from the Jesuit Refugee Service has stated that St. Ignatius, the founder of the Jesuits, would tell us to "act with the generosity of

---

25 Jesuits, "Jesuits Denounce Unjust Treatment of Asylum Seekers and Migrant Families at the U.S. Southern Border, Last modified June 21, 2018, http://jesuits.org/news-detail?TN=NEWS-20180620041409
26 Adriana, Siqueira, "The Spirituality of the 'Spiritual Exercises' of St. Ignatius," *Thought: Fordham University Quarterly* 13, no. 4 (1938): 574–588. doi:10.5840/thought19381344.

Jesus, who gave everything, including his own life, so that others may have life, and have it to the full." I used the word Ignatian in the title because of St. Ignatius's generosity and compassion for the "poor" and "oppressed."

While I do believe that our artistic initiative honors the teachings of St. Ignatius through a practice of consolation, compassion, and discernment in a world that is suffering, I also recognize that to create a more humane and just world that benefits suffering migrants, I must continue to offer more solidarity and accompaniment through different community engagement opportunities.

General Recommendation to Jesuit Universities

Creating indirect opportunities for community engagement, allowed a larger number of students to have a "seat at the table" and offered the opportunity for those who could not physically cross borders to do so in a spiritual way. Participating students reported that this artistic initiative accurately represented USF as a university that values social justice and humanitarianism, and they expressed joy in creating beacons of hope and bridges of solidarity between migrants and the US. This activity fostered a sense of belonging among students and communal hope, helped strengthen campus spirit, and cultivated cooperative action with faith organizations. A limitation of this art activity is that it was not open to communities outside of the university, which limited our ability to learn from community members and to grow our project in terms of the number of participants. Jesuit universities interested in replicating this project should consider opening the event to individuals in the community.

Jesuit universities should also consider collaborating with other faith and grassroots organizations including the Kino Border Initiative, to accomplish successful direct and indirect encounter experiences that benefit migrant communities. In addition, collaborative banners could be created at Jesuit universities in Mexico (e.g., Universidad

Iberoamericana) and Jesuit universities in the US (e.g., University of San Francisco) to boldly emphasize the concept of "cross-border solidarity."

I believe that other Jesuit universities could find great value in promoting social justice issues, like the protection of migrants, through art initiatives. I recommend that this particular art initiative be used at other Jesuit institutions because it has the power to: a) generate student reflection on the collective struggles, strengths, cultural wealth, and resiliency of migrant communities; b) amplify the voices of migrant families fleeing violence, persecution, or extreme poverty in their native land; c) actively underline support for the unification of family members and resistance to abuses against migrant communities; d) and foster the acquisition of a new skill: learning how to create fabric or canvas banners as an act of protest. As mentioned previously, I would recommend that this initiative be open to communities outside of the university to create more inclusive spaces and to invite universities outside of the United States to be co-partners in the implementation of the project.

Conclusion

On May 7, 2018, the Trump administration adopted a "zero-tolerance policy" that prosecutes all unlawful border crossing, making no exceptions for asylum-seekers or migrant families traveling with children. As a result of President Trump's "zero-tolerance policy," approximately 3,000 children were separated from their parents and taken to facilities managed by the Department of Health and Human Services. Unfortunately, the US has found itself unprepared to responsibly meet the physical, psychological, and legal needs of migrant children and their families.

Because the "zero-tolerance policy" is an ineffective policy that is inhumane, heartless, and contrary to Catholic values, Jesuit universities should consider offering direct and indirect (e.g., creating artistic banners of support) community engagement opportunities that communicate love, grace, compassion, generosity, and the social doctrine of the Catholic Church. Jesuit institutions may witness more participation in meaningful encounters from its students, if they offer community-based education with opportunities for indirect contact, rather than just international immersion experiences aimed to help migrant communities. I can confidently say that indirect engagement opportunities can be transformative if they are contemplative in nature and are successful at personalizing migrant experiences through poetry and storytelling (e.g., reading of the poem "Borderbus").

Jesuit institutions can strengthen their presence and advocacy to protect the human rights of migrant children and their families through art initiatives. Art has the power to move large groups of people in subjective ways. To achieve effective responses, Jesuit universities may benefit from building partnerships with both national and international Jesuit institutions. Whatever the activity is and whether it involves direct or indirect community engagement, Jesuit universities have to "practice what they preach" inside and outside of their institution to help strengthen the moral lens of their students and faculty; a moral lens that views migrants as neighbors.

The Artists

The Delivery Team

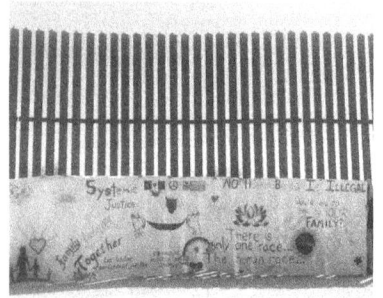

The Message

Learning Interrupted: Deportation as an Educational Policy Issue

GENEVIEVE NEGRÓN-GONZALES[1]

Introduction

In the fall of 2017, I served as the faculty chaperone for a group of students from the Masters in Migration Studies Program at the University of San Francisco (USF) on an educational trip to the Southern Border in Arizona. Hosted by the Kino Border Initiative, a binational migrant-serving organization that works on both sides of the border, we spent three days learning about detention and deportation in the Nogales region, visiting the *comedor*[2] and serving meals to recently deported migrants, and hiking the migrant trail in the Sonoran desert to understand the treacherous and exhausting journey migrants make in their search for opportunity and a better life for their families. It was a transformative experience for the students. As someone who grew up on the U.S.-Mexico border in South San Diego County and had been involved in immigrant rights work since I was a teenager, I imagined the trip would largely involve

---

[1] Genevieve Negrón-Gonzales is Associate Professor of Education at the University of San Francisco. Her work examines the intersection of education, immigration, and inequality. Her co-authored book, *Encountering Poverty: Thinking and Acting in an Unequal World*, was published in 2016 by University of California Press.

[2] soup kitchen

dynamics and experiences that were familiar to me. However, months later, there were two moments that have continued to haunt me.

We visited the women's shelter, a tiny apartment where a small group of women migrants are able to take shelter for short periods of time. These women are at different moments in their migrant journeys - some have been deported and are currently in transit, some will try again to make their journey northwards, and others will stay in the Nogales area, while working in preparation to return to their Mexican home communities. We visited with the women, heard their stories of migration, spent time in their (temporary, transitory) home and admired the handicrafts they made for sale as part of the jewelry cooperative that runs out of the shelter. We sat in a circle, filling the living room of the shelter, and listened to the women's stories of migration. Their children figured prominently in these stories - those they had left behind, those they were trying to reunite with, and those they were trying to care for, sometimes across tremendous distance. I am not a migrant, but I am a mother, and the stories of these women imprinted on my consciousness.

The last day of our trip was spent in the Tucson Courthouse, where we witnessed Operation Streamline court proceedings. Operation Streamline, a joint initiative of the Department of Homeland Security and Department of Justice in the United States, was started in 2005 and is a program that exists only in U.S. border areas. The Operation Streamline model entails rapid prosecution of detained migrants, so that someone who is apprehended over the weekend can be seen in court on Monday morning and be deported by that evening. This model is a part of Immigration Customs and Enforcement's (ICE) "prevention through deterrence" border policy and is made possible because migrants are prosecuted in groups, sometimes shackled and paraded into a courtroom seventy at a time, their deportations ordered in a matter of minutes. First time offenders are deported immediately, and repeat offenders face incremental increases in jail time correlated to the number of crossings. Most of the Operation Streamline defendants are men. What I have continued to turn around in my head since that day are the faces of the women we saw in that courtroom. All young, all "repeat offenders," receiving sentences of thirty, sixty, ninety, 180 days. A question sat in my throat as I watched young woman after young woman come through the court room, each with lengthy sentences. Why cross again and again, risking more each journey, facing higher penalties and longer time in dehumanizing, abusive detention? Though I was not there collecting data and therefore, am not sure my assumption is correct, the only sense I could make of this traces back to what I heard from the women in the shelter. They do it for their children. Their children live here. That is why they continue to cross this border, risking dignity and safety and their lives—to reunite with their children.

For the last fifteen years, I have worked as a researcher, ally and advocate with undocumented young people. The majority of this work has been with college-aged young people - whether they are at a four-year university or a community college. A part of understanding the lives they live as college-aged young people involves understanding where they come from, and how they grew up. In these efforts, I have continued to grapple with how their recollections of their childhood teach us something very important about the cost of deportation on the educational lives of children.

I argue that deportation is an educational issue because of the intense impact that family separation, through deportation, has on undocumented young people and young people in mixed status families. I illustrate this by examining how deportation shapes the financial health of families and how this impacts educational access, how deportation shapes the mental and emotional health of children and how this impacts learning, and how deportation shapes the educational navigations and aspirations of children. I will illustrate this by telling the stories of three young people whom I have encountered in my research; each of their stories demonstrates the ways that deportation, or the threat of deportation, impacted their educational lives. I will conclude by articulating what is at stake for our young people if we do not position deportation as an educational issue, and what is possible if we do.

Deportation and Childhood

That children are victims in the state's deportation agenda is nothing new,[3] though these conversations rarely focus on how deportation intersects with their educational lives. In this political moment, broader conversations about comprehensive immigration reform have been largely eclipsed by a focus on DREAMers and their precarious location as legal outsiders in the country they have grown up in. In the wake of Trump's dismantling of Deferred Action for Childhood Arrivals (DACA), this focus has become even further heightened, exposing the one million young people who have DACA, or are eligible for it, who are caught in a legal limbo with no prospects for comprehensive immigration reform on the horizon. As is evidenced by the attention on the DREAMers, much of the literature on undocumented children examines the educational barriers undocumented young people face in their pursuit of higher education.[4] In recent years, some scholars have included young undocumented children in this analysis,[5] but we have yet to grapple, in a nuanced way, with how deportation shapes the lives of children in this country. We know that there are an estimated one million undocumented children (under the age of eighteen) living in the United States[6] who are therefore vulnerable to deportation. There

---

[3] Dreby, Joanna. "The burden of deportation on children in Mexican immigrant families." *Journal of Marriage and Family* 74, no. 4 (2012): 829-845.

[4] Gonzales, Roberto G. "Young Lives on Hold: The College Dreams of Undocumented Students." *College Board Advocacy & Policy Center* (2009).
Chavez, Maria Lucia, Mayra Soriano, and Paz Oliverez. "Undocumented students' access to college: The American dream denied." *Latino Studies* 5, no. 2 (2007): 254-263.
Manley, Mikia. "More Money, More Problems: The Impact of Tuition Increases on Undocumented Student Achievement." *Chicago Policy Review (Online)* (2016).

[5] Clark-Ibáñez, Marisol. *Undocumented Latino youth: Navigating their worlds*. Lynne Rienner Publishers, Incorporated, 2015.

[6] http://www.apa.org/topics/immigration/undocumented-video.aspx

are another four million undocumented people who have children under the age of 18,[7] thereby also vulnerable under the deportation regime. In recent years, scholars and practitioners have begun to pay more attention to the ways that these young lives are shaped by deportation and displacement, including work on unaccompanied minors[8] and work that examines how immigration policy shapes (and undermines) family life.[9] Nicolas DeGenova's work critically informs this analysis by positing that it is not simply deportation, but also deportability, that shape the lives of migrants living without authorization in the United States.[10] He argues that the accompanying fear and uncertainty that is part and parcel of undocumented life has an impact on all aspects of life whether or not deportation is ever realized. Despite the important work on this issue, as a field – and particularly as scholars of education – we have not yet fully grappled in meaningful ways with how deportation and education intersect. We have yet to make the connections about how living with the threat of deportation, or enduring family separation as a result of deportation, is a pressing dynamic that shapes the lives of millions of children in this country and therefore, is not simply an immigration policy issue, but also an educational policy issue.

---

7   https://www.migrationpolicy.org/article/frequently-requested-statistics-immigrants-and-immigration-united-states
8   Ataiants, Janna, Chari Cohen, Amy Henderson Riley, Jamile Tellez Lieberman, Mary Clare Reidy, and Mariana Chilton. "Unaccompanied children at the United States border, a human rights crisis that can be addressed with policy change." *Journal of immigrant and minority health* (2017): 1-11.
    Oppedal, Brit, and Thormod Idsoe. "The role of social support in the acculturation and mental health of unaccompanied minor asylum seekers." *Scandinavian journal of psychology* 56, no. 2 (2015): 203-211.
9   Dreby, Joanna. *Everyday illegal: When policies undermine immigrant families.* Univ of California Press, 2015.
10 De Genova, Nicholas P. "Migrant "illegality" and deportability in everyday life." *Annual review of anthropology* 31, no. 1 (2002): 419-447.

Methods

The stories I draw from in this article are from interviews that were conducted as a part of the research I have done over the course of the past fifteen years with undocumented young people navigating higher education. For this paper, I draw on three interviews out of nearly 100 that my research assistant and I conducted, because they illustrate the ways in which deportation impacts the financial stability, emotional health, and educational aspirations of undocumented young people. Interviews were conducted for two different research projects: the first, completed between 2007 and 2009, examined the political engagement of undocumented young people, while the second, undertaken between 2013 and 2015, examined the experiences of undocumented community college students in the Central Valley of California. Norma's interview is from the first research project, and Brenda's and Patricia's from the second. Norma was studying at a four-year college and Brenda and Patricia were in community college at the time the interviews were conducted and all were undocumented. Pseudonyms have been used and identifying factors have been changed.

How Deportation is an Education Issue

"Everything is a little chain of more and more problems."

Patricia's Story: Financial Stability as a Casualty of Deportation

Patricia was a promising high school student. The eldest of three children, her parents worked in the fields and were proud to see her excel academically. Patricia graduated high school at the top of her class, but because she is undocumented knew that enrolling in a four-year college would be a financial impossibility. Though she would have been a competitive applicant for four-year colleges, enrolling at her local community college did not feel like a disappointment to Patricia; she was grateful to have the opportunity to continue her education and be a college student. The summer before she started, she was notified that she had been granted admission to the honors program at her college because of her scholastic achievements in high school. Being a part of the honors program gave Patricia priority access to an academic counselor, early registration so she could get the classes she needed in order to ensure that she was enrolling in transferable credits, and other kinds of academic supports like a laptop and textbook loaner program. Patricia's first semester was solid; she earned A's in all her classes and felt confident that she was well-positioned to transfer to a four-year college in a few semesters.

Over the holidays, just after her first semester at college, Patricia's father was detained and deported as a part of an ICE raid at his workplace. Their family of six became a family of five overnight, and the top-wage earner in this family unit was now gone. On top of dealing with the emotional devastation of losing a husband and father, Patricia and her mother were thrust into the panic of trying to figure out how the two of them could earn enough to keep the family afloat. "I mean, he worked in the fields. It's not like he was making so much money or something but you know when you have everything worked out just right, and then his being gone just threw everything out of whack. We didn't have enough money and there was no way for us to have enough." This also happened during the historic California drought, which intensified the problem because it made her mother's work even more insecure than normal. "Yeah the drought was big. They're farm workers. If there is no water, he can't work. Unemployed means, you know, we can't survive. Everything is a little chain of more and more problems." At first, her mother was insistent that this not impact Patricia's schooling; she wanted to find a way for her daughter to stay in school. Midway through the semester, Patricia was promoted to assistant manager at the fast food restaurant at which she worked. The salary boost was something she could not turn down, but she knew that there was no way she would be able to work the increased hours and take on the additional responsibilities without decreasing her school load.

At this point in the semester, it was too late for her to drop her classes so she limped to the finish line, earning several Cs. She was devastated, and in an attempt to be responsible, decided that she would take the following fall off from college so she could work as much as possible to save money for her family and school expenses. She was determined that she would not have another low-achieving semester and that she would not have to choose between work and school. When Patricia returned to college the following spring, she learned that her spot in the honors program had been lost. Unbeknownst to her, participation in the Honors Program is contingent on consecutive enrollment; once you withdraw for a semester you lose your place. This was a big blow to Patricia's plans not just emotionally, but also, pragmatically. With the loss of the honors program, she also lost access to the kinds of academic support that had been so vital to her. She enrolled in classes that were not transferable because by the time she was able to get an appointment with a counselor, there were no other classes available. She went weeks in one class without the textbook because she could not afford it and no longer had access to the loaners. Patricia struggled. She lost her confidence and began to question if college was the right move for her. When I met her, that had all happened three years prior and she was still several classes (and semesters) away from being transfer-eligible.

It is not difficult to see in Patricia's story how her father's deportation impacted the family financially and how her schooling was a logical casualty of that situation. The lines are fairly direct in this case, though for many young people the financial consequences of deportation are more complicated. Time at school means lost wages, which can often look like a lack of motivation on the part of the student when in actuality, the family needs that student to contribute financially. I have spoken with several young people who have given up the chance to go to college so their younger siblings, who are U.S. citizens, can go – it is cheaper for them, as citizens, and the responsibility often falls to the eldest to take on the role of the parent when that role is vacated through deportation. Patricia's situation is particularly clear because she was such a promising student when her academic journey began and we can see how the "little chain of more and more problems" ended up wearing her down and impacting her ability to achieve her dream of a college degree.

"I've never felt at ease. That's hard to carry around every day."

Norma's Story: Deportation and Emotional Health

Norma had a rather sheltered upbringing because her parents worked hard to shield her and her younger sister from the stresses of undocumented life. "I mean, I had chess classes when I was a kid. Like, how many undocumented kids have chess class?" she laughed. Norma's childhood was relatively uneventful, made stable through her parents' regular employment as janitors and a quiet, modest apartment in a lower middle-class neighborhood. When I met her, she was a pre-med college student at a prestigious university. Today, she is in graduate school.

Despite her relatively calm upbringing, her parents did their best to shield her from the stress of their status. Despite her accomplishments, Norma has always struggled with crippling anxiety and debilitating depression. This is not unique among the undocumented students I have interviewed, though Norma's struggles with mental health stand out because her life has been so stable. She attributes her struggles with mental health entirely to her status. She remembers being young and seeing the worry on her parents' faces. "I remember like on the weekends, my cousins would go out and hang out at the mall and stuff, but my dad was always like, mija, let's just stay home, okay?" Her status hung over her like a perpetual cloud. "I've never felt at ease. … When you are undocumented, it's like you are waiting for something bad to happen at every moment. There is always that chance that everything could change. That's hard to carry around every day." The worries increased as she got older and acquired new understandings of what could go wrong. The chief concern that was present throughout these years was the threat of family separation through deportation.

Norma traces her struggles with anxiety to her childhood, talking about how though she knew that her parents worked hard to protect her from the stress that comes along with their undocumented status, the protection in itself caused her to worry. She figured that if she needed to be protected from this thing that felt so all-encompassing and overpowering, that the threat must be real. She recalls repeatedly calling home from the front office in elementary school because she had a stomach ache – it was only in her twenties that she finally recognized that as a symptom of anxiety. While she continued to perform academically, she is clear that her academic performance was an expression of her looking for an outlet outside of home where she had control, where she could get lost in something else, where she could find a refuge from worrying. She is also clear that for some of her classmates, the stress caused the opposite dynamic in school, saying, "I liked school, so that's why it could be a refuge for me. But for some kids, I mean, obviously, you are carrying this all around, school is the last thing you are trying to worry about. It's not that they don't care, it's just that they have too much other stuff going on."

Norma's mental health struggles were not extreme or dramatic – she was never hospitalized, never attempted suicide, and never felt that they impacted her long-term goals or opportunities. But the banal, low-key persistence of these issues in and of themselves is notable; notable in the sense that she had come to see this perpetual uncertainty, the constant knot in her stomach, as a normal part of life that she simply had to accept because she is undocumented. She could not imagine a way out of it, could not imagine another option because there was no way for her to fix her status, no way to rectify this all-consuming problem that shapes every aspect of who she is When talking about the time she considered seeing a therapist, she explains that she dismissed the idea because "I am not gonna pay a lot of money to talk to someone about something neither of us can fix.

There no way to fix this." I asked her to clarify if she was talking about "fixing" her anxiety or her status, and she shrugged, "Both."

"It just makes you afraid of growing or getting out of your comfort zone."

Brenda's Story: Deportation (and Deportability) Thwarting Educational Aspirations

Like Norma, in Brenda's case, it was not deportation, but deportability, that shaped her childhood and educational navigations. Brenda and her family endured a traumatic experience crossing the border – they had to cross three different times because they ended up in detention after their first two attempts. Brenda remembers the trauma of that time, being scared and separated from her father, running through the darkness at three o'clock in the morning with a garbage bag over her head to try to avoid detection from the night vision helicopters that were circling above. The third time they attempted to cross they were finally successful and her family settled into the Los Angeles area before relocating to the Valley. She recalls always feeling like losing her parents was a real possibility because she had lost them, while they attempted to cross the dessert. The trauma was compounded when her smallest sibling, born in the United States, died as a child because of a brain disorder. The fragility of their family unit always felt very close to the surface for her. As I said, it was more deportability rather than deportation that shaped Brenda's life – none of her family members were actually deported but living with the constant fear of deportation and family separation marked her childhood in profound ways.

Brenda recalls how small her world was, as a result of the very palpable fear her parents carried about their status. "There was a little store …we couldn't even walk to the store, it was like just crossing the street. There was a highway, you cross the highway and there was the store where you could buy like popsicles and stuff during the summer.

But we couldn't really, my dad wouldn't drive. He was scared the cops would get him and he would get pulled over and send him to Mexico. My dad would never drive anywhere, only the house to his job and maybe to the grocery store. That's it. We never went to the park. He never took us anywhere. We never went shopping, ever. Everything we had, it was things people gave us or people would sell clothes like on buses and stuff. It was like second-hand clothes. That's what we had. We didn't have like 'oh we went to Walmart'. I didn't even know what Walmart was until I grew up."

When asked about what that meant for her experiences at school as a child, Brenda explains that her family's insularity and fear meant that they had very little connection to her school. "My parents never really went to [parent-teacher] conferences because my dad was always working. My mom never learned how to drive, she still doesn't know how to drive, so my parents never went to a [parent-teacher] conference. If we won an award, we never went to the award assemblies. … I never played a sport because I never stayed after school because I didn't have anyone to pick me up or to take me." Though Brenda excelled academically, her school life was very disconnected from her family life. As she got older and began to think about college, her parents did not actively discourage her, but also did not encourage her. She rushes to clarify that this is not because they are bad people or have some sort of inherent disdain for school. Rather, she says, the fear and uncertainty are so all-consuming that it is hard for them to see outside of it. "I think the fear of getting picked up by the police, it just makes you afraid of growing or getting out of your comfort zone," she explained. Through the course of the interview, I found that Brenda had nearly completed her college credits in order to transfer to a four-year college. I asked her about her plans and was surprised to find out that she had mostly abandoned her plans to transfer. The closest four-year university to her home was an hour away, and much longer (if not impossible) by public transit. Brenda felt that that distance would be hard for her to navigate on a daily basis, and moving was out of the question. "I just couldn't do that to my mom and dad. They'd be too worried. It's not that I don't like it here. I'll probably just stay." She plans to find work in retail. She knows, she tells me, that if she can't find work she can always work in the dairies like her dad.

Conclusion, Significance & Implications

Each of these stories illuminate not only the ways in which deportation (and deportability) shape undocumented young people, but also the ways in which that shapes their lives as students. On the surface, this may seem like an obvious statement. Schooling is a central institution in the lives of all children – most spend more waking hours at school than they do at their own homes. However, when we think about the fact that so many children are grappling with deportation and still, we do not talk about deportation and family separation as an educational issue, it becomes clear that we need to radically reconceptualize the way we think about deportation, family separation, and the educational impacts of U.S. immigration policy.

I insist, in this article, that we need to position deportation as an educational policy issue. In closing, I want to encourage us to think about what it would look like if we did. What would it mean for teachers to be activated around this question and use their moral authority as teachers to refuse to act on behalf of ICE agents, but also insist that there is a moral imperative for them to fight deportation as a force that detrimentally impacts children in their classrooms? What would it mean for teachers' unions to take a strong stand on immigration reform, asserting that the health and wellness of families and children is negatively impacted by deportation policies? What would it mean for schools to see deportation as a community issue, not a private issue that some families have to struggle through on their own, and build support systems to step in when a family in their community has been destabilized through deportation? What would it mean for college presidents to refuse to comply with ICE, citing the protection of their students as fundamental to their educational mission and regarding the operations of the Department of Homeland Security as fundamentally impinging on their ability to carry out that mission? And what would it mean for youth activists and youth workers to stand on a platform of educational rights and educational justice, making it clear that the deportation and immigration policy that so many of them are impacted by is directly impeding their ability to learn and succeed?

    I insist, in this article, that we position deportation and family separation as an educational policy issue and make a case for how it is, but I also want us to think about what is at stake if we do not. Nearly 250,000 people were deported in 2016.[11] That same year, 360,000 people languished in detention centers.[12] The Trump administration has promised to continue to escalate this attack on migrant families, rolling back Temporary Protective Status for Salvadoran, Haitian, Honduran and Syrian people, refusing to reauthorize DACA to protect undocumented young people, taking aim at sanctuary cities, and continuing to execute ICE raids in hundreds of communities across the country. The stakes could not be higher.

    I think about those handcuffed young women we saw in that Arizona courtroom, taking their sentence knowing that once they are released they will risk their lives and their freedom, yet again, because borders cannot keep mothers away from their children. I think about those women in the shelter who speak about the devotion to their children as the reason they migrate. I think about the young men in the *comedor*, getting a meal to fill their bellies and their blistered feet bandaged so that they can continue on their journeys, across continents, through deserts, and traversing borders because their families are waiting. If in our efforts to reform the educational system for this country's children, we cannot see what the deportation crisis is doing to the most marginalized of these families, then we have no hope of enacting real reforms. The time is now for us to act, and those of us in education have not only the moral authority, but also the ethical duty, to protect these children and their families.

---

11   https://www.ice.gov/removal-statistics/2016
12   https://www.detentionwatchnetwork.org/issues/detention-101

The Continued Degradation of Children's Rights in the Trump Era

Emily L. Robinson[1]

Introduction

My client, Mercedes,[2] sits across the table from me in a blue and white Catholic school uniform. Her hair is tied back, but still swirls around her face. She kicks her legs back and forth in the chair, because they can't yet reach the ground. She is eleven years old and has been in the United States for less than a year. Mercedes and her older sister made their journey to the United States "unaccompanied." They presented themselves at the border, were detained, placed for some days in a shelter, and ultimately, released to their mother in Los Angeles. When

---

1   Emily L. Robinson is the Co-Director and instructor for the Loyola Immigrant Justice Clinic (LIJC) at Loyola Law School, Los Angeles. The Loyola Immigrant Justice Clinic (LIJC) is a community-based collaboration of Loyola Law School, Homeboy Industries, and Dolores Mission Parish with a dual pronged mission: to advance the rights of the indigent immigrant population residing on the East side of Los Angeles through direct legal services, education, and community empowerment, while teaching law students effective immigrants' rights lawyering in a real world setting. Since its inception, LIJC has provided consultations to over 10,000 community members and retained thousands of individuals for direct representation. Clinical law students serve as primary advocates for a portion of those clients, and can claim representation for a large number of the Clinic's overall unaccompanied minor client population.

2   Client name changed to preserve confidentiality

they were released, they retained their status as unaccompanied minors. Their mother left when Mercedes was only eleven months old. As a single mother of four, she had to ensure her children had enough to eat and that they could take a bus to school to avoid the gangs known to steal young girls from the part of Honduras where they resided. Once Mercedes' mother left Honduras, all four of her girls were subjected to horrific and constant abuse at the hands of their uncle. Her two oldest sisters fled their uncle a few years ago and were able to apply for and receive a grant of asylum based on the severity of the abuse they suffered. Mercedes and her older sister had to stay behind with their uncle, however, because they were still too small to make the journey.

Cases like Mercedes' are the kind that the Trump administration is trying to ensure can no longer qualify for certain special protections, and, ultimately, asylum based on domestic violence/custodial abuse. This article explores some of the actions taken by the Trump administration to destroy protections for child migrants and shift resources to ensure they are treated and prosecuted as adults.

Background and Protections for Unaccompanied Minors in the Immigration Process

Although child migrants have always fled their home countries in large numbers, the early 2000's saw them fleeing to the United States in increasing numbers. The majority of these children, called "unaccompanied alien children" or "UAC" (hereinafter "UC"[3]) came from Mexico, Honduras, El Salvador, and Guatemala.[4] As is well

---

3 Although the term Unaccompanied Alien Child is a term of art contained in statute, it is perceived by immigration advocates, including myself, as derogatory based on the use of the word "alien." For this reason, this paper uses "UC" preferentially.
4 William A. Kandel, *Unaccompanied Alien Children:* An Overview Cong. Research Serv. Reports (January 18, 2017), https://fas.org/sgp/crs/homesec/R43599.pdf.

documented by various country conditions reports, children fleeing to the United States often have their own, independent protection needs based on persecution, torture and abusive conditions that they faced in their home country. The U.N. Convention on the Rights of the Child states that the primary consideration in all actions involving children should be the best interest of the child.[5] Overall, children are at greater risk of abuse, neglect, violence, torture, exploitation, trafficking, forced sexual abuse, or forced military recruitment due to their age and the lack of protections they are able to access in their home countries. UC children fleeing to the United States are escaping growing violent crime rates, poor economic conditions, high rates of poverty, and the presence of transnational gangs.[6] UC are defined in the Immigration and Nationality Act as children who lack lawful status in the United States, are under eighteen at the time of entry, and are without a parent or legal guardian in the United States or without a parent or legal guardian in the United States who is available to provide care and physical custody.[7]

Two laws and a settlement govern the bulk of U.S. policy for the treatment and processing of UC's. Specifically, the *Flores Settlement Agreement* of 1997; the Homeland Security Act of 2002; and the

---

[5] Convention on the Rights of the Child, G.A. Res. 44/25, U.N. Doc. A/RES/44/25, at art. 3(1) (Nov. 20, 1989), *available at* http://www.un.org/documents/ga/res/44/a44r025.htm.

[6] Congressional Research Report R43628, *Unaccompanied Alien Children: Potential Factors Contributing to Recent Immigration*.

[7] 6 U.S.C. §279(g)(2). *Note* that although children may have a parent or guardian in the United States, that parent or guardian is unable to provide them with the immediate care as required by the William Wilberforce Trafficking Victims Protection Reauthorization Act of 2008, which requires the apprehending agency to notify the Department of Health and Human Services within 48 hours of its "apprehension or discovery" of a UC or within 48 hours of "any claim or suspicion that an alien in the custody of such department or agency is under 18 years of age." TVPRA §§ 235(b)(2)(A)-(B). The federal department or agency must then transfer the UC in its custody to Health and Human Services' Office of Refugee Settlement within 72 hours of determining the child is a UC. § 235(b)(3).

Trafficking Victims Protection and Reauthorization Act of 2008.[8] Although recently revisited due to an ongoing and flagrant lack of compliance, The *Flores Agreement* established a nationwide policy for the detention, treatment, and release of UC and recognized the particular vulnerability of UC as minors detained without a parent or legal guardian present.[9] It requires immigration officials detaining minors to provide them with seemingly basic amenities: 1) food and drinking water, 2) medical assistance in emergencies, 3) toilets and sinks, 4) adequate temperature control and ventilation, 5) adequate supervision to protect minors from others, and 6) separation from unrelated adults whenever possible. It also requires the government to release children from detention at the earliest time practicable and place them in the least restrictive setting.

Thereafter, Congress passed the William Wilberforce Trafficking Victims Protection Reauthorization Act of 2008 (TVPRA, P.L. 110-457)(hereinafter "TVPRA"). This created certain limited rights and protections for UC to ensure safe repatriation, expeditious screening, and the division of responsibilities for UC among various agencies falling under the Department of Justice (DOJ). The Department of Homeland Security (DHS) and the Department of Health and Human Services (HHS) share responsibility for the processing, treatment,

---

8   William A. Kandel, *Unaccompanied Alien Children:* An Overview Cong. Research Serv. Reports (January 18, 2017), https://fas.org/sgp/crs/homesec/R43599.pdf.

9   *Id.* (See DHS Office of Inspector General, *CBP's Handling of Unaccompanied Alien Children*, OIG-10-117, Washington, DC, September 2010). *Flores* has repeatedly been violated by the federal government, leading to a series of lawsuits addressing detention conditions for children in the last few years (*See Flores v. Reno*; *Reno v. Flores*; *Flores v. Sessions*). This is particularly concerning given President Trump's Memorandum dated April 6, 2018 titled "Ending "Catch and Release" at the Border of the United States and Directing Other Enhancements to Immigration Enforcement" which requests immediate steps be taken to end the policy of allowing individuals who present a low flight risk and low risk to the community to wait outside of detention for removal proceedings. This is certain to have a disproportionate impact on children and lead to renewed litigation to enforce the *Flores Settlement*.

and placement of UC.[10] DHS' Customs and Border Protection (CBP) apprehends and detains UC arrested at the border, Immigration and Customs Enforcement (ICE) handles custody transfer and safe repatriation responsibilities and also represents the government in removal proceedings, and the Office of Refugee Resettlement (ORR) coordinates and implements the care and placement of UC in appropriate custody.[11] Congress acted with legislative intent and made a deliberate decision to implement separate and distinct processing protocols for UC apart from those for adults and to vest various responsibilities for UC in different agencies within the DOJ. This was intended to prevent abuses and afford children with special protections tailored toward their unique vulnerabilities and inability to independently navigate our immigration system.

Some of the protections afforded to UC by the TVPRA exempt certain UC's from being summarily removed through the expedited removal process and afford them the right to have their case heard before an immigration judge through traditional removal proceedings conducted pursuant to Immigration and Nationality Act Section 240. Section 240 proceedings allow UC additional time to properly adjudicate their case given their limitations as minors and difficulties articulating the foundation of their claim(s) to legal relief.[12] The TVPRA also exempts UC from the one-year filing deadline in asylum cases[13] and allows them to receive voluntary departure at the government's

---

10 William A. Kandel, *Unaccompanied Alien Children:* An Overview Cong. Research Serv. Reports (January 18, 2017), https://fas.org/sgp/crs/homesec/R43599.pdf.
11 *Id.*
12 TVPRA § 235(a)(5)(D). *See also* Catholic Legal Immigration Network, Inc., "Practice Advisory on Strategies to Combat Government Efforts to Terminate "Unaccompanied Child" Determinations" *available at https://cliniclegal.org/sites/default/files/resources/defending-vulnerable-popluations/Practice-Advisory-on- Strategies-to-Combat-Government-Efforts-to-Terminate-Unaccompanied-Child-Designations-(May-2017).pdf*
13 TVPRA § 235(d)(7)(A).

expense regardless of their ability to pay for repatriation.[14] Perhaps most importantly, the TVPRA provides alternative procedures for the processing and adjudication of UC asylum applications in a way that contemplates the unique sensitivities of children. Despite being in removal proceedings, UC are entitled to file their asylum applications in the first instance with United States Citizenship and Immigration Services ("USCIS") Asylum Office so that they can present their claims in a non-adversarial, interview setting.[15]

De-Designation[16] as an Insidious Tactic to Subvert Legislative Protections for Unaccompanied Minors

Although 6 U.S.C. §279(g)(2) defines what an unaccompanied child is for immigration purposes, there is no statutory or regulatory explanation of what it means to have a parent or legal guardian "available to provide care and physical custody." Statutory timeframes for the processing of children who enter the United States without parents have proved instructive and governed policies that have developed when it comes to making this fact intensive determination. Trump era policies, however, have given us an indication that the practices and policies of the Obama administration, which have evolved over the course of the last decade, will quickly be eroded.

Because the TVPRA sets a firm timeframe on the processing of UC, practice for CBP and ORR has been that a child receives the designation of "unaccompanied" if, at the time the child was apprehended, they were without a parent or if there is no parent

---

14   TVPRA § 235(a)(5)(D). *Note* that voluntary departure is an important remedy when no other immigration legal relief is available as it ensures the immigrant is still eligible for future immigration benefits (such as family-based petitioning) should they later become eligible.
15   TVPRA § 235(d)(7)(B); *see infra* Section III.B.
16   *As of the date that this article was submitted for review to USF's Lane Center, dedesignation continues to evolve as to the anti-immigrant, anti-UC policies of the Trump administration.

immediately able to receive them upon arrival. The child is then transferred to the care of ORR even if they have a parent in the country who the child might eventually be released to. It has been USCIS guidance and practice that once a child has been designated as a UC at entry, they continue to be so classified even if they no longer squarely fit the definition (for example, if a child attains the age of eighteen or reunifies with one or both parents upon entry into the United States).[17]

On January 25, 2017, President Trump issued his Executive Order titled "Border Security and Immigration Enforcement Provisions," which instructed the Secretary of DHS to take "appropriate action" to ensure that UC are properly processed. Thereafter, on February 20, 2017, John Kelly issued a memorandum titled "Implementing the President's Border Security and Immigration Enforcement Policies." This memorandum touches on UC in several sections. Section L of the memo is entitled "Proper Processing and Treatment of Unaccompanied Alien Minors Encountered at the Border." Specifically, the memo states:

> Approximately 60% of minors initially determined to be "unaccompanied alien children" are placed in the care of one or more parents illegally residing in the United States. However, by Department policy and practice, such minors maintained their status as "unaccompanied alien children," notwithstanding that they may no longer meet the statutory definition once they have been placed by HHS in the custody of a parent in the United States who can care for the minor…To ensure the identification of abuses…the Director of USCIS, the Commissioner of CBP, and the Director of ICE are directed to develop

---

17 *See e.g.,* Ted Kim, "Updated Procedures for Determination of Initial Jurisdiction over Asylum Applications filed by Unaccompanied Alien Children" (May 28, 2013) stating that "unless there was an affirmative act by HHS, ICE or CBP to terminate the UAC finding before the applicant filed the initial application for asylum, Asylum Offices will adopt the previous DHS determination that the applicant was a UAC" *available at https://www.uscis.gov/sites/default/files/USCIS/Humanitarian/Refugees%20%26%20 Asylum/Asylum/Minor%20Chil dren%20Applying%20for%20Asylum%20 By%20Themselves/determ-juris-asylum-app-file-unaccompanied-alien-*

uniform written guidance and training...regarding the proper processing of unaccompanied alien children.[18]

The memorandum then goes on to instruct the agencies (USCIS, CBP and ICE) to establish standardized review procedures to ensure individuals initially designated as UC continue to meet the definition found at 6 U.S.C. §279(g)(2). By requesting the review of the UC designation, the memorandum is requesting a procedure by which various agencies can act to withdraw or terminate UC status, and, with it, accompanying statutory protections. The reason is to ensure that child migrants are not improperly availing themselves to the legal protections afforded to UC in the removal process.[19] This concept will hereafter be referred to as the de-designation of UC status.

The immediate concern of advocates was twofold 1) fewer children would initially be classified as UC at apprehension and instead, would be removed pursuant to expedited removal processes, and 2) children who were classified as UC at entry, would either formally or informally be stripped of that designation causing them to be forced to adjudicate asylum claims before the Executive Office for Immigration Review (EOIR), be subject to expedited removal, no longer eligible for voluntary departure and lose access to federally funded programs for legal representation, among other benefits.[20]

Despite the call for coordinated, inter-agency policies, the first agency with explicit guidance to de-designate has been EOIR. On September 17, 2017, Jean King, General Counsel, issued a memorandum titled "Legal Opinion re: EOIR's Authority to Interpret the Term Unaccompanied Alien Child for Applying Certain Provisions of TVPRA." This memo provides legal guidance to EOIR on the issues of

---

18 John Kelly, "Implementing the President's Border Security and Immigration Enforcement Improvements Policies," (February 20, 2017).
19 *Id.*
20 Immigration Legal Resource Center (ILRC), "Unaccompanied Minors & New Executive Orders," (March 21, 2017) *available at https://www.ilrc.org/sites/default/files/resources/uacs_under_trump_administration_final_3.21.17.pdf*. These concerns become all the more valid in light of President Trump's Memorandum dated April 6, 2018 titled "Ending "Catch and Release"

1) if DHS' initial determination of UAC is binding on the immigration court and 2) whether an individual who previously held status as a UC, but no longer meets the definition, continues to be entitled to TVPRA protections. The memorandum reads as though it is trying to force a legal concept using deductive reasoning. The memorandum supports its own conclusion by finding that because EOIR is mentioned at various points in the TVPRA and charged with aspects of the UC removal process, the DHS' UC determination is not binding on an immigration judge. Thus, the memorandum reasons, immigration judges have authority to "resolve any dispute about UAC status" during removal proceedings or when it becomes relevant to a respondent's eligibility for relief or ability to file an initial asylum application with USCIS.[21] The memorandum cites *Matter of Herrera Del Orden*, 25 I&N Dec. 589 (BIA 2011) to assert that immigration judges are charged with all aspects of a removal proceeding unless withheld by an act of Congress. No such articulation to withhold jurisdiction or authority from EOIR is present in the text of the TVPRA with the exception of jurisdiction over initial asylum applications for children who *are designated as UC at the time of filing*.

While it *may*[22] be a valid legal conclusion that immigration judges have legal authority to de-designate, it is certain that the TVPRA does not list ICE or EOIR as entities with the authority to make determinations regarding UC status deliberately. There are a

---

21 Jean King, "Legal Opinion re. EOIR's Authority to Interpret the term Unaccompanied Alien Child for Purposes of Applying Certain Provisions of the TVPRA," (September 19, 2017). *See also* Catholic Legal Immigration Network, Inc., "Immigration judges' authority to review "unaccompanied alien child" (UAC) determinations," *available at https://cliniclegal.org/resources/immigration-judges-authority-review-unaccompanied-alien-child-uac- determinations.*

22 Arguments (not discussed in this paper) can be made that EOIR and ICE actually lack the authority to strip a UC of their designation based on a close statutory interpretation of the TVPRA which requires that CBP and ICE either find that a child is "unaccompanied" and transfer him or her to ORR within 72 hours, or notify ORR of any child under eighteen within 48 hours. TVPRA § 235(b)(2).

few reasons that it is unlikely Congress intended for immigration judges (or other agencies not charged with making the initial UC determination) to be regularly reassessing UC status. The TVPRA is meant to afford children, meeting certain criteria at the time of entry, with protections. Undoubtedly, EOIR has jurisdiction over removal proceedings, however, Congressional intent is clear. Their goal was to slow expedited removal of children and protect them by giving primary responsibility to ORR, an agency better positioned to understand the unique needs of children and to care for them in a setting where their health, educational and emotional needs could be met until a UC could be placed with a qualified parent or guardian. Congressional intent to charge ORR with primary responsibility for UC is consistent with the overall legislative intent of the TVPRA as ORR holds "comparative institutional expertise in making child welfare determinations (as is required in deciding whether a parent or legal guardian is available to provide care for a child), in contrast to the lack of expertise in other federal agencies."[23]

In enacting the TVPRA, Congress wanted to impose a firm timeframe for the processing of children so that they would not languish in immigration detention.[24] It considered complex trauma and its impact on the mind of a child and saw that the asylum office was better positioned to use a child-sensitive lens and avoid re-traumatization than the traditional, adversarial court setting when evaluating claims for asylum put forth by UC. Congress also wanted to do away with a one-year filing deadline because authors realized that it can take children prolonged periods of time to navigate our immigration system, locate legal representation, and develop the confidence to articulate the basis of the past persecution they suffered

---

23 Catholic Legal Immigration Network, Inc., "Practice Advisory on Strategies to Combat Government Efforts to Terminate "Unaccompanied Child" Determinations" *available at https://cliniclegal.org/sites/default/files/resources/defending-vulnerable-popluations/Practice-Advisory-on- Strategies-to-Combat-Government-Efforts-to-Terminate-Unaccompanied-Child-Designations-(May-2017).pdf*

24 TVPRA § 235(b)(2).

adequately to satisfy the requirements for a grant of asylum pursuant to Immigration and Nationality Act Section 208.[25] Therefore, it can be extrapolated that by vesting different aspects of UC processing in different agencies, without articulating a process for divesting any individual agency, Congress realized that in many ways, EOIR is not the agency best positioned to determine the needs of children, and, even EOIR itself, and the regulations the agency previously put in place, offered enhanced protections in removal to ensure the relief applications before EOIR were adjudicated with the "best interest of the child" as the paramount consideration.[26] While the Jean King memorandum states that implicating EOIR in the TVPRA means the agency has authority to take away UC designations, Congress certainly could not have contemplated the DOJ stripping TVPRA protections away at the first practicable moment.

Treating Children as Adults and Fraudsters is the Only Legitimate Goal of De- Designation

The Kelly and King Memoranda, both explicitly and implicitly stand for the same proposition, that UC violate our immigration system and we should proactively investigate them to ensure that they are

---

25 TVPRA § 235(d)(8) directs that UC asylum cases be governed by regulations that consider the specialized needs to UC and which address both procedural and substantive aspects of handling UC cases. *See also e.g.,* Ted Kim, "Updated Procedures for Determination of Initial Jurisdiction over Asylum Applications filed by Unaccompanied Alien Children" (May 28, 2013) *available at https://www.uscis.gov/sites/default/files/USCIS/ Humanitarian/Refugees%20%26%20Asylum/Asylum/Minor%20Chil dren%20Applying%20for%20Asylum%20By%20Themselves/determ-juris-asylum-app-file-unaccompanied-alien- children.pdf.*

26 Operating Policies and Procedures Memorandum (OPPM) 07-01, "Guidelines for Immigration Court Cases Involving Unaccompanied Alien Children," (May 22, 2007). *Note* that this guidance was rescinded and replaced on December 20, 2017 by OPPM 17-03 which has a tone significantly less favorable to children and no longer mentions the "best interest of the child" as a consideration for judicial discretion.

not robbing us of a benefit to which they should not be entitled. In the EOIR context, de-designation is exceedingly problematic for a number of reasons and is likely to lead to disparate and fundamentally unfair outcomes. For example, individual immigration judges vary drastically in their use of discretion and the way that they apply the law. Depending on the individual immigration judge and their desire to reevaluate a UC designation, certain UC will be disproportionately harmed. Another variable is the degree to which the ICE Office of the Chief Counsel Trial Attorney, assigned to any individual case, attempts to advocate for the stripping of UC status by filing motions or notices to terminate or by pressuring the court to terminate UC status. Further, overall EOIR approval rates vary drastically by jurisdiction, which shows the climate and bias of each region.[27] It can be assumed that the more conservative courts will be the same courts that are more inclined to reevaluate a UC designation. It is exceedingly unjust that a child located in California is more likely to be able to proceed in their removal case with TVPRA protections in place, while an individual in a less immigrant friendly state will increasingly lose those protections.[28] It stands that Congress acted deliberately when affording children

---

27 For example, according to the U.S. Department of Justice, Executive Office for Immigration Review FY 2016 Statistics Yearbook, in the year 2016, San Francisco had 74% approval rate for asylum applications, whereas Salt Lake City, Utah had a 7% approval rate. https://www.justice.gov/eoir/page/file/fysb16/download

28 For example, the Catholic Legal Immigration Network, Inc. has begun gathering reports of attempts to de- designate and has already received reports from jurisdictions in Michigan, Ohio, Texas and New York of trial attorneys and/or judges instructing children who have reunified with one parent to file applications with the immigration court as opposed to the asylum office, and, of ICE trial attorneys filing "Notices of Termination of UAC Status," with the immigration court. *See* Catholic Legal Immigration Network, Inc., "Practice Advisory on Strategies to Combat Government Efforts to Terminate "Unaccompanied Child" Determinations" *available at https://cliniclegal.org/sites/default/files/resources/defending-vulnerable-popluations/Practice-Advisory-on- Strategies-to-Combat-Government-Efforts-to-Terminate-Unaccompanied-Child-Designations-(May-2017).pdf*

protections, and the fact that a child turns eighteen does not ensure that they are able to understand our immigration process in a superior way on their birthday.

The EOIR Memorandum, coupled with the Kelly Memorandum, is likely a harbinger of policy to come. The Jean King Memorandum opens the door for other agencies to use their access to UC and resources to de-designate. The Kelly Memorandum seems to contemplate routine re-evaluation and reclassification of UC by calling for standardized review procedures to ensure a child, initially determined to be a UC, continues to fall within the statutory definition found at 6 U.S.C. §279(g)(2).[29]

At present, the March 28, 2013 USCIS policy for processing asylum applications has not been rescinded, and, therefore, individual asylum officers are instructed to accept a previous UC designation and not reevaluate. However, the Kelly memo could lead to USCIS officers asking questions during the course of an asylum interview to determine if a child has reunified with a parent, has a guardianship in place or has aged out of protections or a particular social group such that they would not qualify for asylum. If the asylum office engages in an additional, secondary inquiry into UC status, it is possible that they will begin rejecting applications filed, and decline initial jurisdiction for children who have been released to parents or have turned eighteen prior to filing. Further, wait times for the adjudication of UC asylum applications has only grown since President Trump took office. It may be possible that the asylum office attempts to deny an asylum application on the basis

---

29 John Kelly, "Implementing the President's Border Security and Immigration Enforcement Improvements Policies," (February 20, 2017). *See also* Catholic Legal Immigration Network, Inc., "Practice Advisory on Strategies to Combat Government Efforts to Terminate "Unaccompanied Child" Determinations" *available at https://cliniclegal.org/sites/default/files/ resources/defending-vulnerable-popluations/Practice-Advisory-on- Strategies-to-Combat-Government-Efforts-to-Terminate-Unaccompanied-Child-Designations-(May-2017).pdf.*

that a UC turned eighteen during the time the individual awaited a decision on the merits of their claim.

ICE could also take proactive steps to de-designate. Although it is uncommon for children, in the adult context, ICE officers schedule regular check-ins with immigrants assigned to their case load. Typically, these meetings are to verify that nothing about an individual's case has changed and to hold the immigrant accountable. ICE officers have the power, however, to require their UC clients to attend check-ins as well. Officers may attempt to use these meetings to evaluate if the child's situation has changed such that they no longer fit the UC definition. They may then feel empowered to prepare a notice to terminate UC designation, and may even desire to take a UC into DHS' custody for detention purposes. Whether it be ICE, USCIS or EOIR who de-designates, the effect will be the same—that children who have located a guardian or reunified with a parent (or, alternatively, attained eighteen years of age) could be forced to proceed with their asylum applications before EOIR in the first instance, lose access to Section 240 proceedings and become subject to expedited removal, or no longer be able to pursue asylum, as a remedy all together, due to the passing of the one-year filing deadline. It could also cause certain individuals previously considered UC to be taken into DHS detention as *Flores Settlement* protections would no longer attach.

This shift by the Trump administration also opens the door for new policies and practices by various agencies in the DOJ to determine whether a child is unaccompanied at the point of entry. This could have far reaching ramifications. Policy may evolve in such a way that if a child enters alone, and does not have parents "available to provide physical custody" pursuant to the previous interpretation, but does have a parent or legal guardian somewhere in the United States, they are deemed "accompanied," and subjected to expedited removal (or other removal short of §240 removal proceedings) on this basis and/

or detained in DHS facilities as opposed to being released to ORR, an entity better positioned to care for children.[30]

It is important to emphasize that this policy shift will not just impact children that attain eighteen years of age, but also children like Mercedes who has been reunified with her mother after receiving a UC determination. A child of eleven certainly should not be forced to testify regarding the abuse she suffered and her fears of being forced to become a "gang girlfriend" before a judge and trained trial attorney. Her reunification with her mother does not make it so that she is not the kind of child Congress Is desirous to protect.

So why does the Trump administration want to act in clear contravention of Congressional intent and in a manner that appears to circumvent legislation? It is certainly not to protect children in the manner Congress intended when it enacted the TVPRA. It also cannot be to alleviate court resources as compelling immigration judges to oversee the litigation of all asylum claims will further strain already overburdened immigration court dockets. Certainly, Congress vested initial jurisdiction for asylum applications with USCIS and provided associated asylum protections because USCIS has the capacity for greater specialized training and provides an environment where the adjudicator can use non-adversarial interview techniques to illicit the facts necessary to receive a grant of asylum. The division of jurisdiction also promotes efficiencies in determining eligibility for an asylum benefit. If de-designation continues to proliferate, legal representatives for any UC will oppose de-designation, further impacting court dockets. Taking UC into DHS custody adds to already crowded detention centers and generates increased costs for tax payers (especially where the

---

30 Catholic Legal Immigration Network, Inc., "Practice Advisory on Strategies to Combat Government Efforts to Terminate "Unaccompanied Child" Determinations" *available at https://cliniclegal.org/sites/default/files/resources/defending-vulnerable-popluations/Practice-Advisory-on- Strategies-to-Combat-Government-Efforts-to-Terminate-Unaccompanied-Child-Designations-(May-2017).pdf*

child is a minor and has enhanced emotional and educational needs). The only logical basis for this policy shift is that this administration has adopted and consistently developed a rhetoric and discourse that unaccompanied children are fleeing to the United States for no legitimate reason other than to take advantage of our resources. This is further fueled by the discourse by the Trump administration that children from Central American countries are gang members and/or are putting forth fraudulent asylum narratives.

These policies also speak to a shift in priorities for the current administration. As opposed to ensuring children are protected with the full force of legislation, the government is engaging in a close read of the plain language of the TVPRA to find any justification to deprive children of rights and benefits to which they are entitled. This places additional pressures on child migrants, and creates enhanced barriers to success on the merits of their potential claims for immigration relief.

Strain on Nonprofit Resources in the Struggle to Best Serve Child Clients and Unique Challenges in the Clinical Teaching Setting

It remains to be seen how extensively de-designation will be used, but the policy shift has already had a far-reaching impact for nonprofit legal service providers representing UC. We understand that two potential events may cause an individual to fall outside of the statutory definition of UC: 1) reunification with a parent or the appointment of a guardian and 2) attaining eighteen years of age. Advocates have been in close communication on a national level to track when ICE or an immigration judge takes action to de-designate. The Kelly Memorandum stands for the proposition that it may not be necessary for action to be taken for a UC to lose their status, but, instead, may not fall within the definition as a natural consequence of one of the two events described. Catholic Legal Immigration Network, Inc. maintains a tracking form for advocates to report when the government has taken steps to remove UC protections.[31] This form inquires as to the steps the government used in their attempt to de-designate as well as the result (expedited removal, inability to file for asylum affirmatively by government opposition or rejection by the asylum office and DHS detention).[32]

Although there is no set mechanism or procedure to de-designate, advocates can use a variety of tools to improve their client's chances of retaining TVPRA protections. If a client is nearing eighteen years of age, one potential strategy is to file an asylum application with the asylum office prior to the client's birthday. This increases the chances that the office will accept initial jurisdiction. For a client who has reunified with a parent(s), it is best to file the asylum application before any upcoming master calendar hearing to vest jurisdiction with the asylum office before the government or immigration judge can attempt to de-designate.

Certain clients who are eligible for asylum are also eligible for Special Immigrant Juvenile Status ("SIJS"), which is codified at 8 U.S.C. § 1101(a)(27)(J).[33] A SIJS predicate order, which must be obtained in State Court, can be obtained through delinquency, dependency or a child custody (parentage) action. If an advocate chooses to pursue SIJS, it is safest if an asylum application is filed prior to seeking the appointment of a custodian or guardian in State

---

31 Catholic Legal Immigration Network, Inc., "Tracking UAC De-designations," *available at https://cliniclegal.org/tracking-uac-de-designations.*
32 *Id.*
33 The TVPRA also amended SIJS and clarified the requirements to qualify for this status. To qualify, a juvenile court must have jurisdiction and make certain findings of fact: 1.) a child (defined as an individual under 21 years of age) who is not a citizen or national of the United States must be legally committed to, or placed under the custody of, an agency or department or an individual or entity, 2.) reunification with one or both parents is not viable due to abuse, abandonment, neglect or a similar basis under state law and 3.) it is not in the child's best interest to return to his or her home country. The applicant cannot be married at the time of filing the SIJS petition or when the petition is adjudicated, and must be present in the United States at the time of filing. 8 U.S.C. § 1101(a)(27)(J).

Court. While TVPRA § 235(d)(5) expressly protects children from losing UC protections when seeking protection from a state court, it is possible that a judge or ICE trial attorney might argue that a child is now accompanied due to State Court SIJS findings, and, therefore, ineligible to file an asylum application as a UC.[34] Advocates might also seek to protect their clients by fiercely litigating judicial determinations or trial attorney actions to de-designate, but it may take federal court litigation to prevail, which can be time consuming and cause clients stress, uncertainty and even deportation during the pendency of the case. Another strategy may be to seek continuances or termination of a removal case, based on a pending application, to avoid an opportunity for an immigration judge or trial attorney to allege a client has lost UC protections.[35]

There may be instances in which an advocate suspects that a client is eligible for asylum, but has clear SIJS eligibility. De-designation may cause advocates to quickly file for asylum before fully assessing eligibility to preserve all options for a client. All of the above presented strategies are resource intensive and time consuming. Many UC clients go unrepresented, however, the majority of clients with counsel have been retained by non-profits without the time or financial ability to pursue multiple remedies for all clients, especially in cases where eligibility is unclear or has yet to be determined. This becomes particularly difficult in the law school clinical teaching setting. Students in immigration clinics like LIJC are encouraged to lawyer in "slow motion." The goal of such clinics is to ensure students are competent in their interviewing and counseling skills before entering practice. They are also challenged to research heavily and engage with the full breadth of applicable law. De-designation may lead to

---

34 Catholic Legal Immigration Network, Inc., "Practice Advisory on Strategies to Combat Government Efforts to Terminate "Unaccompanied Child" Determinations" *available at https://cliniclegal.org/sites/default/files/resources/defending-vulnerable-popluations/Practice-Advisory-on- Strategies-to-Combat-Government-Efforts-to-Terminate-Unaccompanied-Child-Designations-(May-2017).pdf*

35 *Id.*

a decrease in UC representation by law school clinics as students are not always ready to file cases in the strategic order presented above. In Mercedes' case, clinical law students had to employ child-sensitive interviewing techniques and build trust with their eleven-year-old client before she provided them with the facts necessary to support an asylum claim. It quickly became apparent, however, that she was eligible for SIJS and that the SIJS State Court process could be completed in the course of a semester. The question for educators becomes how to balance pressures placed on advocates by the new administration with acceptable outcomes for student learning. It is also important to engage students in the external pressures driving case strategy so their timelines comport with compelling client needs and the goal of zealous advocacy.

Conclusion

The Kelly and King Memoranda display a distressing trend. It is certain that children's cases will continue to take exponentially more resources as new border security measures and policies for interior enforcement evolve. The Trump administration is displaying its desire to use procedures and administrative policies to circumvent legislative protections built up over the course of the last decade. Federal litigation is necessary to articulate that using agency procedure in contravention of Congressional intent is improper and in violation of the law, as well as coordination on the part of non-profits and law school clinics to bolster their resources in the face of increased challenges.

The Undocumented Truth: Uncovering Stories of *La Perrera*, Trauma, Human Rights Violations, and Separation of Children and Families Coming out of a South Texas I.C.E. Detention Center

BELINDA HERNANDEZ-ARRIAGA[1]

Dicen que a muchos nos crearon
En algún lugar del continente Asiático
Todos hechos gracias por mano de obra barata,
Y Por alguna razón del destino terminamos aquí
En suelo Centroamericano
Lugar donde vuela con libertad el pájaro Quetzal
con su pecho rojo y plumas de jade
Donde la baleada, la pupusa y las catrachas fueron creadas
Pues dicen que donde uno nace,
Uno ahí deja su espíritu y en otro lugar renace

---

1 Belinda Hernandez-Arriaga, Ed.D., L.C.S.W. is Assistant Professor at the University of San Francisco in the School of Education's Counseling Psychology Department. With twenty years of working in the field of mental health, her advocacy and immigration support are centered on the psychological implications of deportation, separation, and inhumane immigration policies for immigrants.

Esta es una carta de despedida
Para mi querido amiguito
Pero no me puedo despedir
No sin antes contarles sobre nuestro peregrinaje y como nos conocimos

Llegué a tu vida en una caja y en forma de regalo
Juntos estuvimos en eventos importantes
Juntos fuimos a la escuela, a la iglesia y a fiestas familiares
Fui tu sostén y en mi pusiste todo tu peso
Y te cargue, como una madre carga a su hijo (2x)
En cada paso siempre estuve contigo

Juntos recorrimos y conocimos muchos lugares
Y cuando decidimos emprender este camino
Tuve miedo porque no sabía lo que nos depararía el destino
Juntos huimos de todo peligro
Cruzamos Montañas
Y Cruzamos Ríos
Cruzamos Praderas
Y también Fronteras
Y Nada, Nada
Nada nos detuvo

Jamás nos dimos por vencidos
Y en momentos difíciles continuamos nuestra marcha
A paso lento, pero firme
Y cuando tus pies se cansaron
Otros brazos nos ayudaron
En cada paso siempre estuve contigo

Es muy triste tener que decir Adiós mi querido amiguito
Ahora que hemos llegado aquí
Al destino deseado
No me quiero despedir
Pero entiendo que es momento de un nuevo comienzo
Que para soñar no hace falta caminar

Adiós querido Amiguito
Espero que tu próximo compañero

Te lleve a buen puerto
Hasta aquí llega nuestro camino
Y Que Dios bendiga cada uno de tus pasitos

Atentamente, con mucho amor y cariño

English Translation:

They say that many of us were created
Somewhere in the Asian continent
All done thanks to cheap labor,
And for some reason of fate we ended up here
On Central American soil
The place where the Quetzal bird flies freely
with his red chest and jade feathers
Where the food dishes of the *baleada*, the *pupusa* and the *catrachas*
were created
Well, they say that where one is born,
One leaves his spirit there and he is reborn in another place

This is a farewell letter
For my dear Little friend
But I cannot say goodbye
Without first telling you about our pilgrimage and how we met

I came to your life in a box and in the form of a gift
Together we were at important events
Together we went to school, to church and to family parties
I was your support and you put all your weight on me
I carried you, as a mother carries her son (2X)
In each step I was always with you

Together we traveled and visited many places
And when we decided to take this road
I was scared because I didn't know what destiny would bring us
Together we escaped all danger
We crossed Mountains
And we crossed Rivers
We crossed Prairies

And also Borders
And Nothing, Nothing
Nothing stopped us

We never gave up
And in difficult moments we continued our journey
Slowly, but firmly
And when your feet got tired
Other arms helped us
I was always with you in every step

It's very sad to have to say Goodbye my dear little friend
Now that we have arrived here
To the desired destination
I do not want to say goodbye
But I understand that it is time for a new beginning
That to dream one does not need to walk

Goodbye my dear Little Friend
I hope that your next friend
Will take you to a good place
Up to here is the end of our road
And may God bless each of your little steps

Sincerely, with a lot of love and affection[2]

TU ZAPATITO![3]

With determination to make it to *El Norte*[4] to escape violence and seek asylum, worn-down *zapatitos*[5] have walked long journeys to borders that will give them hope for survival. The journey of Central Americans to the United States, captured by media images during the summer of 2018, covered the United States' forced separation of children from their parents. The cries of mothers, fathers and children,

---

2   Poem by Julio Valenzuela, volunteer with Bay Area Border Relief
3   YOUR LITTLE SHOE!
4   The North
5   little shoes

as well as the harrowing stories of the caravan, pushed Americans to be in solidarity with the immigrant community. Against the backdrop of racism and the criminalization of immigrants fleeing their countries, allies and caring community members joined together to offer *apoyo*[6] to the children and families making the long journey to the U.S. for safety. The journey from Central America to the U.S. is a difficult one, but families and children embark on it because they are "driven by a kind of blind faith, born of desperation, that this is their best chance to escape the poverty, violence and hardship they knew at home and to build better lives. The first thing they need to do, they say, is to get to the border" (Semple, Koreal, Avrbuch 2018). In the summer of 2018, the treacherous journey for families and children turned into an escalating trauma that put their lives in peril. Trump's attacks on immigrants rose to new levels as he implemented a heartless policy of separating children and parents at the border for an indefinite amount of time and with no plan.

Trump's aggressive political decision to traumatically separate children from their parents was a visible national tragedy that continues to paralyze immigrant families. Aaron Hegarty of USA TODAY reported on April 6 of 2018:

> Attorney General Jeff Sessions announces a "zero tolerance" policy at the southwest border. It directs federal prosecutors to criminally prosecute all adult migrants entering the country illegally. The policy change leads to the separation of families because children cannot be held in a detention facility with their parents.

Individuals around the country were frozen with disbelief upon seeing desperate parents crying to be reunited with their children. Many mothers and fathers empathized with immigrant families, imagining their own experiences of having their children forcibly taken away. Allies, activists, organizations, politicians and caring individuals mobilized to stand against the policy at the Southern Border. Raices, a Texas non-profit immigration legal center, raised twenty million dollars from donations around the country to fight the separation of

---

6   support

children and families. As the country rallied to stop the separation of children, politicians also joined in the movement and spoke out against Trump's actions.

With voices growing louder against the inhumane policy of separating children, on June 20, 2018, Hegarty relayed:

> Facing a national outcry, Trump signs an executive order designed to keep migrant families together at the U.S.-Mexico border, abandoning his earlier claim that the crisis was caused by an iron-clad law and not a policy that he could reverse. The order, drafted by Nielsen, directs [Department of] Homeland [Security] to keep families together after they are detained crossing the border illegally. In addition, Homeland reports 2,342 children were separated at the border from 2,206 adults from May 5 to June 9.

As the national politics spiraled out of control and helplessness for the children pushed us to action, one Bay Area community came together to provide direct resource support and care to immigrant families in the aftermath of the separation. A U.S. congressional delegation of twenty-six, along with U.S. House of Representative Jackie Speier, responded to the separation crisis with a visit to the South Texas Border. Representative Speier invited her Bay Area team of 12 activist women, who were known as the "McAllen 12," to witness the crisis unfolding. Their purpose was to witness— and speak out against— the separation of children from their parents. "Frankly, what we really want to do is go in that building there and hug those children, but we know that's not possible," said volunteer Lilli Rey. "Rey and her Bay Area humanitarian group raised 1,000 pounds of clothes and toys to donate to shelters serving migrant children in McAllen" (Jennings, 2018). Representative Speier was able to go into the detention center and witness the experiences of young children housed in the facilities alone. She, along with the team of twelve women, shined a light on the humanitarian efforts needed at the South Texas Border. The group came back to the Bay Area determined to mobilize others.

After spending a year responding to the crisis and working with victims, a team of faculty and graduate students, from the Counseling

Psychology program in the School of Education at the University of San Francisco (USF), were invited to join the McAllen 12 team of women. Rooted in USF's mission to "change the world from here," a team of ten came together to serve at the South Texas Humanitarian Center. This *testimonio*[7] reflection captures the undocumented stories that were heard as we helped families with showers, served them their first meal out of Immigration & Customs Enforcement (I.C.E.) detention, and gave them *zapatos*[8], clothes, and words of care to support the next phase of their journey. For us at USF, our work was to not only be witnesses, but to also be allies to the migrant families who had endured so much along the way. In addition, our presence represented a direct action against the inhumane policies that ushered them into *los Estados Unidos*[9]. Our team carried the slogan of *"Estamos Contigo*[10]*"* to demonstrate our care to those we would welcome with hope and *amistad*[11]. Our work came at the end of the separation policy and at the beginning of the chaos to unite children with their families, many of whom are still separated today. The social justice mission was based out of the Catholic Charities Humanitarian Respite Center in McAllen, Texas and the local Greyhound bus stop, which the New York Times calls the "New Ellis Island" (Manny, 2018). Over the course of five days, we shared sacred space in the humanitarian center with babies, children, youth, parents, *abuelitos,*[12] and dads to welcome them with care into the U.S. Evenings were spent at the bus station translating, providing education about bus routes, and giving supplies to the families to make their long bus rides to their family sponsor easier. For the team, the five days spent with the children and families were emotionally challenging as there were tears, concern, fear and hope that each of them would find their way

---

7 testimony
8 shoes
9 the United States
10 We are with you
11 friendship
12 grandparents

in *El Norte*. This reflection captures the work I did as faculty to guide the journey of our USF team.

Our Journey to the South Texas Catholic Charities Humanitarian Respite Center

Once immigrants cross into the United States in the Valley and are apprehended by law enforcement, they are typically taken to the U.S. Border Patrol immigration processing center in McAllen. If the immigrants are seeking asylum and have a family member or sponsor living in the U.S., agents release them to the respite center.

Workers at the respite center temporarily take them in — often not overnight — to feed, bathe and care for them until they usually board a bus at the McAllen bus station to join their family member or sponsor. The immigrants then await their date in immigration court, where an immigration judge will either grant or deny their asylum claim (Ferman 2018).

Every day the Respite Center receives individuals, children, and families who have been released from I.C.E. detention. The Respite Center staff and volunteers are the first to welcome those who are exhausted and confused as they step onto U.S. soil after being in custody. On one particularly busy day, the center staff asked a few of us to receive the individuals coming out of I.C.E. at the bus stop, where they are released for the first time since being apprehended. As I walked to meet them, my heart raced realizing that I would be the first to greet them and welcome them to this country. When I arrived, I saw a line of mothers, young children, fathers, little ones holding their hand, *abuelos*[13]*,* and *abuelitas*[14]. I saw tired faces, blank stares, fear, and most of all, people holding on for another day in a country they believed was *unido*[15], to welcome the stranger. What they found was the opposite. I wondered what they saw in my eyes.

---

13 grandfathers
14 grandmothers
15 united

Did I represent those who had taken away children or the policy that vilified them as criminals? Did I remind them of someone who refused to feed them with care or of someone who had given them an ugly stare? Holding back the tears, I felt so grateful to have this moment with them; I opened my arms and greeted them with a smile. "*Bienvenidos a nuestro país, estamos contentos que estan aquí*[16]," I said. As I slowly outlined the basic needs that would be fulfilled at the center, I heard gasps when I shared that they would be able to take a shower. One mom and daughter hugged with surprise when they found out they would shower soon. I did not quite understand the depth of their reaction to showering until I was at the shower stations where they began to share story after story of how long they had not bathed. As we walked the four blocks to the center, little ones grasped their mother or father's hand tightly. Mothers hugged their babies, and fathers scanned their surroundings, all of them not sure where they were going or what to expect at their next stop. Exhaustion and confusion were visible in their eyes as they entered the humanitarian space. They trusted us without understanding where they were. As the door opened, some of the staff applauded, welcoming them for the next twenty-four hours they would be there.

Zapatitos, Little Shoes

After the individuals checked into the center and did paperwork, it was time for them to begin preparing for their shower. Each of them only had the clothes they journeyed with since leaving home. Even in I.C.E. detention they are not given any change of clothes. Therefore, the clothing donations that come from around the country to the Respite Center are critical. These donations are organized and separated into stations. As volunteers, we were all assigned stations to provide resources and help each individual passing through. There was the food station, the shower station, the clothing room, the

---

16 "Welcome to our country, we are happy that you are here."

shoe closet, the children play space, and the large *sala*[17] area where everyone gathered. Each space became sacred with the stories that were shared.

I stood in the crowded shoe closet, welcoming each child and parent that waited in the doorway with a pair of shoes with laces (in I.C.E. detention, they remove the shoe laces of each individual). One dad held the hand of his three-year-old son as he handed me his little shoe that fit in the palm of my hand. He told me, "*Mi hijo camino trienta dias para estar aqui, aveces lo podia cargar en mis brazos pero el tambien tuvo que caminar.*"[18] Holding his little shoe in my hand, I realized that I held an untold journey of a family crossing *fronteras*[19] to survive. Fear and desperation drive individuals and families to make this journey and leave everything behind. No one makes this journey unless they are forced. Each time I heard someone's story, my heart was moved as I saw the strength and fear in their eyes. In that shoe closet, I saw hope; I saw *mamás, papás, familias, niños y niñas, hermanos, hermanas y gente de gran corazón.*[20] I saw moms like me; a dad that carried his child with love like my father carried me as a little girl. I saw the grace of elders that sat in silence. I saw my daughters in the little girls her age that lined up for shoes, hoping to get a sparkly one that was buried deep down in the pile. I saw young boys wishing they could be playing soccer outside, but cramped in a space waiting to eat their first meal. I held muddy shoes that were drenched with sweat and tears as they were forced to run further and further from home to survive. In a closet of *zapatitos*, I saw humanity and the face of Jesus in each person and child I met.

---

17 room
18 My son walked thirty days to be here, sometimes I was able to carry him in my arms, but he also had to walk.
19 borders
20 mothers, fathers, families, boys and girls, brothers, sisters, and people with great heart

The Shower Station, *Los Baños*[21]

Two of our students were assigned to be at the shower station. They were asked to help give towels, explain where the hygiene supplies were, and assist the women with what they needed for their showers. During one of my rounds, I was able to assist and witness the complicated emotional process of a shower. Just as with the *zapatitos*, once the women were greeted with a smile or heard the volunteers conversing in Spanish, they began to share emotional stories with us. Each of them recounted how many days had passed since they had last showered; for some, it was up to ten days since showers in I.C.E. are not regular or routine according to those we helped at the center. As they waited for the shower, they all struggled to cut their jeans over the ankle bracelet that had been put on them during their I.C.E. detention stay. Some cried with our team because they felt it was too tight and were desperate to loosen it. Others shared that it rubbed against their skin, and they requested long socks so it would not cause an open wound. One mom was not able to take a shower because she did not want to cut the only pair of jeans she had. The supply room quickly turned into a space of tears and frustration as the women realized the implications of the ankle bracelet that had just been placed on them a few hours earlier during their court proceedings to request asylum. We watched them feel helplessly trapped by an ankle monitor that would track their every move.

One by one as they took their showers, a sound stood out to the volunteers of our team. As they each came out of the private showers, they let out a deep sigh, almost collectively, as if the water freed them in some way. Days after we left the humanitarian center, their permeating sighs rang in my spirit. Was it the sigh of humanity or a sigh that honored the water as a representation of freedom, a baptism of life or a cleansing of the injustice so many had endured on the journey? Did they breathe out the human rights violations and traumas they experienced or was this a sigh of hope? As we handed

---

21 the bathrooms/the Shower Station

them their toiletries, we hoped that during their time with us, they would feel safe.

La Sala de Comida,[22] The Dining Room

During the five days I spent at the humanitarian center, one of the spaces I observed regularly was the area where we would feed the children, mamás, papás, and others. Our team served them bowls of warm soup prepared with love by the humanitarian center. I observed one five-year-old so hungry he got sick after eating too many bowls of soup. There were several other children whom experienced the same tummy issues of being so hungry they would eat too much. As moms rushed to get their children fed, we heard stories of the deplorable food conditions in I.C.E. detention. One mom shared that her daughter had stopped eating because she found a worm in her sandwich. Another shared that they were fed frozen sandwiches every day, and they had *asco* or feelings of wanting to throw up. Little ones were thirsty, and several parents shared they were dehydrated. One mom explained that they repeatedly asked for medical care in I.C.E. due to dehydration, but were never seen. We rushed to get them *suero*[23] out of the medical supply office to feel better. As we fed them one by one, I saw a hunger that was invisible. It was not a visible hunger, but a silent hunger that had been there all along. I saw tears as some families ate; others wanted to ask for more, but did not know if they would be turned away. I saw the inhumanity and unfairness of life that forces poverty on some, while others increase in wealth with each stock market bell ring. My heart ached, and I rushed to pack as many sandwiches as I could for their long bus trip to their sponsors. Only then did I realize that for them sandwiches had become a trauma trigger, a reminder of their time locked up in I.C.E. and separated from one another. The sights, sounds, and smell of the detention center lingered in their bread.

---

22   The Dining Room
23   Pedialyte

On the wall in the dining hall was a large picture of Santo Toribio Romo González, a Patron Saint for immigrants crossing the border. Years before, I had traveled to Mexico to visit Santo Toribio's church in Santa Ana, Mexico, where he had been a priest during the time of the *Cristeros*.[24] He was killed for celebrating mass and working with the children to bring catechism and faith to the community. Long after his death, immigrants crossing the border began receiving help from an unknown individual who would present himself during near-death border crossings. Stories of Santo Toribio indicated that he would show lost immigrants the way; appear in the desert with water for them to drink when they could not go any further; and even walk them to safety. Walking by his photo on the wall, I prayed that somehow Santo Toribio would give these families a home here in the U.S.; protect them; and help them find their way on this difficult journey. His eyes pierced the room as each family ate its food in silence, waiting to move onto the next station of the Respite Center.

The Children, *Los Niños*

During late evenings, our team would debrief on what we experienced and heard during the day. One particular night, we sat in silence, anger, and disbelief as we exchanged stories about *La Perrera*.[25] Holding a sacred space for the stories that the families shared, our conversation focused on the continued separation of children from their parents in detention. Julio, one of our team members who spent his time working with the children, shared that the youth spoke to him about their days in *La Perrera*, a cage in their country known to house the most vicious animals. Numerous children described in detail the traumatic time they spent together not knowing if they would see their parents again. Over the course of our time with them, we heard similar stories of the youth being housed together night and day with no parental visits and no play time; in fact, they were

---

24 Catholic faithful during the Cristero War
25 Detention cages

reprimanded if they left the cages to talk to one another. The youth shared complicated stories of not knowing if it was day or night in detention because of the florescent lights. The only way they could tell the difference was through a small hole in the fan where they would catch a glimpse of light. While the media cameras reported Trump's revised policy to reverse the separation of children from their families at the border, we witnessed the silence around the ongoing, unjust process of separating children ages ten and up from their parents who remained in I.C.E. detention.

On the second day at the bus stop, I observed a mother who sat in a chair in silence, holding her daughter's hand with tears. She sighed and looked up to talk with me when I asked if I could help her with anything. She explained that she missed her youngest daughter who she had to leave behind in Honduras, but hoped her time here would allow her to work to send money for food she did not have. She also shared her hope that she would be able to join her someday. As we spoke, her ten-year-old daughter, who wore a Disneyland t-shirt she received at the humanitarian center, hugged a teddy bear she had also been given. I asked mom how she was doing and tears flowed down her face. She shared that they had been separated in I.C.E. detention for five days and felt scared. Her daughter looked at me while mom shared the story, waiting for my reaction. I reached out to hold her hand and explained she was safe with mom now, while holding down the anger that welled up in my throat.

Everything stood still in the humanitarian center when we saw a little girl running back and forth from room to room repeatedly asking for her mamá. We saw the desperation in her eyes, and her voice began to get louder as she yelled out for her from one space to the next. As her desperation grew, each of our team members began to notice and started to help her find her mamá. I grabbed her hand, and after we moved through the kitchen, the *zapato* closet, the shower center, and finally, the bathrooms, we ended up outside. As fifteen minutes passed, which seemed like hours in the small space, the little girl started breathing harder, and her anxiety clearly increased. It was an escalated fear I had not observed in a child in a long time.

Minutes later, we realized there was a bathroom in the *sala* area we had not searched. Pushing the door open and yelling her mother's name, we heard her mother reply, *"aquí estoy!"*[26] She ran with relief to her mom, and the tears stopped. I stood in silence as I realized that I had just observed the fear that so many children were carrying at their core: the reality that at any given moment they could permanently be separated without warning. For one brief moment, I lived this cruel fear though the eyes of a child and wondered where she would tuck away these emotions until the next time.

Psychological Implications for Children

Separating children from their parents and putting them in cages is an unnecessary trauma that has long-term mental health impacts. As a result of my counseling profession and work to help children address traumatic experiences, I often hear stories of abuse.

I have spent years writing and developing a clinical definition of *unodocutrauma*. This trauma is one that is centered on chronic societal fear, regular fear of deportation or separation of family due to deportation, heightened experiences of racism and/or chronic stress, increased anxiety related to status in the U.S. and emotional stressors related to being undocumented or mixed status.

> While it is clear that trauma exists in this community and can be categorized into varying subsets of clinical definitions of trauma, there is not one trauma that specifically accounts for the intense and pervasive, ongoing fear of being undocumented. In addition, the combination of fear, accumulated emotional stressors of political criminalization, racism targeted at immigration status, and the psychological symptoms of threats or physically being separated from one's family are not addressed in other trauma categories. While we can adapt and fit the symptoms these children experience in other categories, it is imperative that the mental health field address this specific trauma of our youth (Hernandez-Arriaga p. 169, 2018).

---

26 I am here

After hearing the stories of the children and youth in the center, I began to rethink the definition of *undocutrauma* to include the forced separation of children from their parents who are refugees seeking asylum. This government-inflicted trauma is clearly a deep wound that will have a long-lasting impact on child victims and their parents in their effort for survival.

The separation of families through forced deportation, Trump's policy of separating children and families at the border, and the ongoing separation of children in I.C.E. detention are traumas that should be addressed in this population of children and families.

Nuestros Manos y Corazones,[27] A Call To Social Justice Action

As our time was coming to an end in South Texas, our team made a commitment to the center that we would continue to provide support. Seeing the refugees' escalating need for resources, as well as emotional support, left us wishing we could be there long-term. One of the statements a staff member made reminded us of how invisible their agency is against the backdrop of activism happening in our country. He explained that after the lights of the media dimmed and supplies stopped coming in from around the country, the Catholic Charities Humanitarian Center would still be there to welcome refugees fleeing to survive. They still need donations, and there is still lots of work to be done to recognize and embrace each individual as a gift in their struggle to survive. As we left, we knew there would be more children to sit with, more families to feed, more mothers to console, and more walls to break down. In addition to understanding the importance of gathering resources for the center, we internalized the need for ongoing human rights advocacy. During our time there, we texted attorneys and looked for ways to fight against the human rights violations shared with us. We connected refugee families to ongoing services in their area, as well as food, clothing, and monetary support

---

27 Our Hands and Hearts

from others who asked to partner with them. As we returned home, we all agreed to combine our team of USF faculty and students, and the McAllen 12, into one group called Bay Area Border Relief.

Collaborating with faculty across USF's School of Education and other departments, our hope is to develop a platform of advocacy to develop research and support and influence policy around immigration actions and reforms. On the mental health side, our Counseling Psychology program is exploring critical factors of *undocutrauma* in our immigrant communities and rethinking how we provide care for refugee families seeking asylum. Around the Bay Area, caring communities of individuals and groups have rallied to raise funds and gather resources for the Catholic Charities Humanitarian Respite Center. As a community, our belief is that we can break down borders through opening our hearts with *cariño*[28] and using our hands to welcome each individual for who they are. We will not accept the criminalization of a community struggling for survival nor will we accept the destruction of their character through calls to build a wall. Our value is in building *esperanza*;[29] in seeing Jesus in their eyes; in healing the wounds of hate. Our work at the border was a reminder that we are all one. Let us welcome those who embark on the journey with *unidad*.[30] *Caminamos juntos y adelante.*[31]

---

28 Affection
29 Hope
30 Unity
31 We walk together and onward!

No Need to Fear; We're American

JULIO E. MORENO[1]

With labels like "illegal alien" painting me as either criminal or a drain on this nation's economy, I understand why compassionate Americans have negative views of undocumented immigrants and even fear our presence. Events like 9/11, the 2008 economic downturn, fear of the United States losing its worldwide clout to a rapidly rising China, as well as a decline of America's heart and soul—its middle class—within the last twenty years have understandably heightened fear and uncertainty. Collectively, these events have exposed unprecedented vulnerability.

Pressed into fear and uncertainty, Americans responded by mobilizing on the left and the right. Mobilization on the right gave rise to the Tea Party and ultimately, placed President Donald Trump in the White House. Trump and ardent anti-immigrant advocates have unfortunately capitalized on concerns of hard-working Americans. They demonize undocumented immigrants, press for bitterly divisive policies, and have stubbornly blocked legislation that would legalize

---

1 Dr. Julio E. Moreno is Professor of History at the University of San Francisco. He is the author of multiple articles and books, including *Yankee Don't Go Home,* a book on his broader research interest in U.S. business, diplomacy, and culture in Latin America—a line of research inquiry he continues in his current book on the history of Coca-Cola in Latin America. Dr. Moreno has also worked as a consultant, held various leadership posts, and served as an analyst and commentator for NBC-Telemundo and Univsión television stations in the San Francisco Bay Area.

the status of millions of immigrant families—the very own families that have either fed or cared for your children. More recently, the Trump Administration has thrown the weight of the Attorney General to directly separate immigrant children captured at the US-Mexico border from their families. Though the Administration has presented family separation as a basic enforcement of law, such policy, and the dark picture of undocumented immigrants Trump and others project, is misguided and misleading. Most importantly, they are divisive and dramatically hinder our ability to collectively address the unprecedented challenges we face as a nation. As my personal experience in this essay illustrates, undocumented immigrants—their work ethic, integrity, and their unwavering determination to fight adversity—are a constructive force in America.

The story of how my family and I climbed into America's middle class started in the Salvadoran countryside, and it was a result of my mother's courage and resilience. She brought me into this world at our modest home in the village of Cutumay Camones with the help of a midwife, and economic necessity forced her return to work three days after my birth. This type of poverty generally characterized daily life in early 1970s Camones. However, our family situation took a turn for the worse in 1971 when my father was brutally killed—leaving my mother with two children and six months into a third pregnancy. My younger brother died shortly after birth. Emotionally devastated, but determined to move forward, my mother focused on feeding us. She worked a small plot of land our father left us and raised chickens and pigs to make ends meet.

Things improved in the mid-1970s when my mother remarried and gave birth to my fourth brother, Alvaro. My stepfather, Jose Abrego, also owned a small plot of land, and he took the lead with agricultural work with my brother, Francisco, and me at his side. We worked the land in the morning and went to the local village school, Jose Alejandro Cabrera, in the afternoon. The corn and beans our family grew from March to October supplied basic staples, and good harvests often left extra grains, which my mother sold in the city. My mother also tried to always have a cow so that my brothers and I always had milk. Starting in late November, the whole family migrated to coffee plantations for the harvesting season. We typically spent three months picking coffee at the Buenos Aires finca—a coffee plantation owned by the Regalado family, one of the fourteen families that dominated the nation's coffee industry.

For my mother, the crops we grew and the money we earned during the coffee harvesting season represented a significant improvement from the bitter poverty she had once known. Born in Camones as an illegitimate child in 1944, she recalls days as a little girl when my grandmother could not afford food. As a village fruit vendor with two small children in the late 1940s, my grandmother could make enough money to buy corn and beans. On good days, they could only afford to eat maicillo-made tortillas with lemon and salt. Maicillo is a grain inferior to corn typically used as pig's feed in Camones. The bad days brought hunger and uncertainty. My mother still breaks down as she recalls days when she was unsure if a daily meal would be available.

Considering my mother's experience, I understand why she taught my brothers and me to take pride in our work, to be thankful for what we had, and to relentlessly pursue our dreams. Her dream in the 1970s was for us to work in an office—any office job that would not involve getting our hands dirty. Poverty and the 1980's civil war placed limits on these dreams. Teachers traveled from Santa Ana city to Camones daily and began to return home earlier in the day as violence escalated. Morning work limited school attendance to the afternoon, and their earlier departure reduced education to less than three hours a day.

The unprecedented violence and traumatizing fear that accompanied village life during the war far exceeded the poverty my mother had previously experienced and gave her the courage to migrate to the United States. The Salvadoran military and the leftist FMLN guerrilla group often fed out of young recruits—as early as 13 years-old—from the countryside, and my mother feared both. In our quest to get an education and learn a trade, Francisco and I had begun to take the village bus every morning from Camones to the City of Santa Ana. In my case, I was learning carpentry at a woodshop in Santa Ana in the morning and then, took the bus back to village school. This increased risk of recruitment into the violent conflict. The Salvadoran military typically stopped the local village bus, "La Camoneña," on its way to the city and literally dragged young men from the bus into military service. The fear that my brother and I could be recruited into the military—not poverty—gave my mother the courage to migrate to the United States.

If fear gave my family the courage to leave the village, a transnational coyote network connecting Camones to the east LA neighborhood of El Sereno facilitated migration. My stepfather first used this coyote network in the early 1980's to come to the United States and then, used the same network to bring my mother and my seven-year old brother, Alvaro, in 1983. The next year, my parents had saved enough money to bring Francisco. I left on February 3, 1985. The coyote network my family, and most people in the village used, was allegedly headed by a ringleader described by everyone as a white lady in her fifties who lived in San Diego.

This network had another Camones resident and me fly from El Salvador to Tijuana and arranged for us to stay at a hotel. I was told to act and speak "Mexican," Spanish with a different intonation, when I arrived in Tijuana. I failed miserably at this, but Tijuana residents were welcoming. An older, prosperous man saw that we looked lost at the airport and generously offered to take us to the hotel. Though we both tried to act Mexican, he knew we were heading north and advised us to be careful.

I broke the law for the first and only time in my life when I crossed the border on February 6, 1985. We were picked up by the coyote network from the hotel in downtown Tijuana at 11 p.m. and taken to the fence near Playas, where we joined a larger group. At the fence, another coyote helped us cross onto the U.S. side of the border at midnight and led us into a four-hour walk. We ended up in someone's backyard at 4 a.m. and stayed there for an hour until a car arrived. The driver packed five of us in the trunk and told us to remain calm. He took us to a house where we joined twenty-five other people in a small room for two days. It was crowded, but we had food, water, and a television set to Univisión all day. At 4 a.m. on February 9, a separate group of coyotes, two white males in their twenties with long-hair, packed eight of us in an RV. They sat in the front seats, closed the curtains, and played loud rock music as they drove to LA. At around 7 a.m., they collected $450 from my parents and delivered me to a small and already crammed studio we could barely afford in the east LA neighborhood of El Sereno.

Life in America was good even though I did not speak a speck of English. There was also the issue of getting over culture shock. I will never forget the awe I felt when I visited a supermarket for the first time. I was enthralled at the sheer quantity of food available in light of the fact that I grew up without refrigeration. My first warm shower was thrilling – I was amazed at the availability of hot water. Unfortunately, my first hamburger was disappointing…after a lifetime of hearing about this amazing American delight, I was disappointed to find that the mighty hamburger was, in my view, simply a piece of meat with bread.

Predictably, finances were always a concern. Except for my little brother, everyone in my family was working in factories for $3.25 an hour. I started working at the same factory, Farwest Bed Frame, with Francisco. To get around child labor laws, and as a favor to my family because we needed the money, the factory supervisor hired me to work full time under someone else's name. After attending Wilson High School from 7 a.m. to 3 p.m., I clocked in at 4:30 p.m. and ended work at 1 a.m., only to barely start my homework at that time.

I stopped making bedframes when Farwest went out of business, but started working on maintenance for a contractor that cleaned offices at the Sears Building in Alhambra. I moved from cleaning offices to bussing tables at Chef's Take Out, a family-owned BBQ restaurant, after the Sears Building closed down. Chef's Take Out, like Farwest, went out of business, but the job loss came at a good time. Francisco and I had taken Saturday Bank Teller Classes at East Los Angeles Occupational Center, and I was fortunate to land a job at Security Pacific Bank. Though job changes came as a result of the changing nature of American industries in the 1980s, I was fortunate to gradually land better-paying jobs that my mother had always wanted for us. I remember her pulling me aside at my high school graduation and telling me that her dream of having Francisco and me get an education and working at an office—the bank—had come true.

Bank of America ended that dream when it purchased Security Pacific and terminated my job, but this turned into a long-term career opportunity in education. My senior year in high school included tutoring English as Second Language (ESL) students, and this led to a job offer as a Teaching Assistant at Wilson High School just as I was starting my first year at Pasadena City College (PCC). My work as a teaching assistant paid for my stay at PCC and the two years I spent at Cal State L.A. Most importantly, teachers and mentors at Wilson High School helped me discover my passion for education.

No individual could possibly travel my journey alone, and it would have been impossible without the support of my educators. Among others at Wilson High School, Bill Rumble made a long-lasting impact on me. I remember the day when he pulled me aside to express his belief in my academic potential and asked if I was considering attending college. With a full-time schedule at Farwest, I was neither a star student nor did I think attending college was possible. I was barely getting a "C" in his class. His comment gave me desperately needed confidence and steered me into thinking of college. It also triggered a mentorship that proved critical throughout high school, my work as a Teaching Assistant, and my undergraduate education.

Other mentors also played a critical role in my journey. At Cal State L.A., Timothy Harding, Donald and Marjorie Bray, Gloria Romero, and Carol Srole encouraged me to apply to graduate school after commenting on the quality of my work assignments. Without much planning, I decided to apply to graduate school. I ended up applying to History graduate programs at Stanford and the University of California in L.A., Irvine, Riverside, and San Diego. Stanford and UCLA automatically rejected me because of my scores on the Graduate Entrance Exam (GRE). This was expected, as I did as poorly on the GRE as I had done on the SAT, where I scored a combined total of 580. My 3.23 high school GPA was good enough to have gone directly from high school into Cal State L.A., but my SAT score had eliminated that possibility. The dismal standardized testing scores shook my confidence, but made encouraging comments, from mentors who could see beyond my testing scores, more valuable. Two of those mentors were Steven Topik and Peggy Garcia Bockman at UC Irvine. Upon my acceptance to UC Irvine, Topik and Garcia Bockman informed me that I had been accepted into the History Graduate Program and received a yearlong Graduate Opportunity Program (GPOP) fellowship.

Attending graduate school at UC Irvine was the most intimidating experience of my life. I moved into campus housing in the summer of 1992, just as my family pulled all our savings together to purchase our first house in Pasadena. To fight my own academic insecurity, I spent the summer months reading from about 8 a.m. to the early morning hours the next day. Thanks to the GPOP fellowship, I continued this reading schedule during my first year, except for the time I spent in the classroom. The long hours I spent reading did not make discussions at graduate seminars any less intimidating. Comments by other students, who did not hesitate to flash their esteemed undergraduate programs and speak of their parents' academic credentials, stood in stark contrast to mine, and ultimately, impacted my self-esteem. My SAT and GRE scores and my community college undergraduate route simply did not do much to boost my self-esteem. My parents' academic background didn't fare well when compared to that of other classmates, either. My mother was fortunate to be literate, but my stepfather was not. He, like most children in the countryside in the 1950's, started working at age six and never attended school. Fortunately, I found comfort in their example and the values I had learned from them: Work hard, be resilient, and never give up.

Things improved after my first year of graduate school. Aware that my immigration status eliminated the pursuit of most funding opportunities, Peggy decided to hire me as a coordinator for graduate student services. This job essentially extended my GPOP fellowship stipend and was strategically designed to build professional leadership skills among underrepresented students. As I worked in graduate student services, I became more confident in my own abilities. I learned that other graduate students often faced the same insecurities and challenges, though rooted in different personal experiences. In fact, part of my job consisted of organizing events and services to help students navigate the rigorous graduate school experience. I also joined others in the development of a graduate student organization, the Graduate Student of Color Collective, aimed at creating a community of mutual support for underrepresented graduate students. The community we formed also proved critical to my graduate school experience, as it fostered confidence.

Academically, I worked closely with Topik, and he instilled the confidence I desperately needed. Keenly aware of my personal background, he saw my work ethic and helped me channel my raw academic potential into a path that allowed me to successfully navigate rigorous graduate school requirements: Qualifying exams, dissertations, research proposals, and job applications, among others. I finished the Masters Program within a year, finished qualifying exams by the end of the third year, and was the first in my cohort to finish the dissertation in 1998 despite having to switch my dissertation topic. I initially wanted to write a dissertation on the militarization of Salvadoran society throughout the twentieth century, but my immigration status did not allow me to travel abroad. To get around this, Topik and I worked closely on selecting a dissertation topic I could research from the United States. This led me to research, publications, and expertise on the study of U.S. business and diplomacy in Latin America.

Besides the knowledge and professional experience I gained at UC Irvine, I also worked as a teacher at Santa Ana City College. I was initially hired at a satellite campus to teach high school subjects for adults. This campus also offered ESL and citizenship classes, and I started teaching there shortly after California voters passed Proposition 187—a prelude to recent anti-immigration laws in other states. Prop 187 radically increased the number of legal residents who applied for U.S. citizenship in the mid-1990's, and my job was to coach these students to pass the citizenship exam. Working with these students remains one of my most rewarding experiences. Most were in their fifties and came energized to learn English and Civics after a long, arduous workday. We learned, laughed, conducted mock citizenship interviews, and celebrated when students announced they had passed the exam.

As I celebrated the good news, my own immigration status stood on shaky ground—a Temporary Residency Program (TPS) the U.S. Government had extended to Salvadoran residents since the early 1990s. The U.S. Government adopted this program in response to domestic pressure from the Central American Solidarity Movement. Initially centered on opposition to American foreign policy in El Salvador, this movement criticized U.S. immigration for denying over ninety-seven percent of Salvadoran political asylum cases. It accused the U.S. government of denying these cases because accepting refugees who were fleeing a U.S.-backed right-wing government directly undermined America's Cold War policy in the region.

Whatever the reason, TPS opened a window into the pursuit of my dreams. The program authorized Salvadorans to legally stay in the United States, but had limitations. Legal residency was temporary, but it was typically renewed every eighteen months if accompanied by an application and processing fee. Though the program authorized legal residency, it prevented me from traveling abroad. This was the reason why Topik and I had to find a dissertation topic I could research in U.S. archives. TPS allowed me to legally work and attend college without having to pay out-of-state tuition. However, it prevented me from qualifying for much needed financial assistance. As a result, I had no option other than working either two or three jobs that often added to over forty hours per week.

The work ethic and relentless commitment to get an education paid off. The first reward came in March 1996 when I became a legal resident through suspension of deportation. This program required that I put myself through deportation procedures in order to get a court hearing where an unfavorable ruling translated into deportation, but a favorable one gave me permanent legal residency.

The court hearing was memorable and heartfelt. Family, students, fellow graduate students, and Topik all packed the courtroom and cheered as the judge ruled in my favor. Legal residency gave me the opportunity to travel to Mexico for my dissertation research, which I finished in 1998. The completion of my Ph.D. program that year came a decade after high school, and it also came with a job offer at the University of San Francisco (USF). The rewards and milestones continued in 2001 when I officially became a U.S. citizen, and in 2003, with the publication of my first book and promotion to tenured Associate Professor.

The opportunities I found in this country, the mentorship of compassionate Americans, and the work ethic I learned from my mother made my journey possible. I was fortunate. Keenly aware of this, I have been passionately committed to supporting those who have motivation and drive to pursue an education. This commitment started when I began tutoring ESL students at Wilson High School and grew with my graduate student service work and role as a high school and citizenship teacher. At USF, I have spearheaded activities to broaden the learning experience and engage students in community service by designing and teaching courses on sustainable development that include summer-long community service in Latin America, Africa, and Asia. I have also expanded my role as an educator to bring multiculturalism to the social studies curriculum in California public schools. I worked with Harcourt Publishers on a social studies book series that incorporates into a grand historical narrative the story of how various groups within American history have collectively played a critical role in the making of this great nation. This includes the story of how immigrants from all over the world have historically served as a source of strength, not a weakness, to this nation.

My experience is a testament that despite the fear associated with the presence of undocumented immigrants in America, their values and work ethic continue to be a source of strength. It captures the various functions hard working immigrants perform and the newfound patriotism we embed into our work. As a child in the Salvadoran countryside, I picked the coffee Folgers delivered to American consumers. As a recent teenage immigrant, I built the bed frames for American families to enjoy their rest, even as such labor drastically limited my own rest. As a graduate student, I trained new citizens in American Civics, despite my own legal residency status hinging on a temporary program. As a college professor, I continue to educate the future generations of this country. As a researcher and scholar, I am determined to re-conceptualize the way we understand American business and diplomacy abroad in an effort to make U.S. capitalist expansion a source of domestic strength and a mechanism for upward mobility for people across the world.

If my experience points to the patriotic and constructive nature of immigrants, why have anti-immigrant groups been so successful at painting the presence of others in this country in such a negative light? As this essay has shown, part of the answer to this question lies in the uncertainty and fear that America's heart and soul—its middle class—has experienced in the last two decades. Anti-immigrant groups have exploited this uncertainty to successfully push for policies and attitudes that cast a dark shadow over America's very own strength and identity. That strength rests on our work ethic, our reliance to push forward despite adversity, and a relentless determination to pursue our dreams. These are the qualities my family and I, like other immigrants, have brought to this nation. In other words, you have nothing to fear; we are as American as you are.

www.ingramcontent.com/pod-product-compliance
Lightning Source LLC
Chambersburg PA
CBHW031138090426
42738CB00008B/1132